FLYOVER NATION

FLYOVER NATION

You Can't Run a Country
You've Never Been To

DANA LOESCH

SENTINEL

SENTINEL
An imprint of Penguin Random House LLC
375 Hudson Street
New York, New York 10014

ISBN 9780399563881 (hardcover)
ISBN 9780399563898 (e-book)

Printed in the United States of America
1   3   5   7   9   10   8   6   4   2

Designed by Cassandra Garruzzo
Set in Sabon LT Pro

Dedicated to my mother, Gale; her mother, Beulah; and the rolling Missouri hills that raised me. Also thanks to the other great women in our family: Gale Loesch, Modena Loesch, and Mary Drury.

CONTENTS

FLYOVER NATION

Introduction

In the summer of 2004, as I was juggling a baby and freelancing on the side, President George W. Bush was barreling toward reelection. Democrats were beside themselves that Teresa Heinz Kerry's uncharismatic housewife, John Kerry, couldn't run away in the polls against a man they hated with every ounce of their withered, coexist-bumper-stickered souls. Not only were conservatives still popular, but President Bush's wartime brand of God-fearing Midwestern conservatism gathered applause at every campaign stop (though the big spending and expansion of government would later tarnish his legacy due to Tea Party criticisms).

That's why they pushed a near nobody named Thomas Frank onto the best-seller list and kept him there for nearly five months with a book called *What's the Matter with Kansas?* Frank had traveled around his family's home state trying to discover why liberals were not popular in a state where Democrats had ruled a century before. His book got some things right, like the disconnect between many Republicans in

Congress and the citizens they claimed to represent. He got bigger things wrong, however, like his thesis that those citizens would eventually realize their opinions were all wrong and would turn into progressives exactly like him.

What's remarkable about the book, though, isn't where he ended up; it's where he started. The coastal city dwellers knew so little about people in a state like Kansas that they were eager to read the ramblings of anyone willing to go there and translate. They were as curious and ignorant as Columbus sailing for the New World, and those coastals turned a book about malls and cornfields and cities too small for Minor League Baseball fields into a best seller.

This book is just one example of a media strategy we've seen employed countless times before and since: Send a reporter out to 'Murica and see if he can explain what the heck these people do without Cuban-Indonesian fusion restaurants, appletinis, juice bars, and SoulCycle.

This would all be funny if the coastal elite didn't run this country.

Whenever coastal snobs lecture the rest of America about a problem that requires social engineering, that problem resembles what the rest of us call "real life."

Growing up, I never viewed church as some sociological, political force, some graceless entity that required containment, something that extended beyond a simple moral code that every successful society needs to achieve success. Church was the place we heard the preacher tell us that despite our imperfections, we were still loved. It was the place that dispatched a shepherd of God to hold my grandmother's hand when she was too proud to weep and make it right with Jesus in front of her family on her deathbed. It was the place where people came together after my grandmother died and cooked hot meals for my family, who were too distraught to think of much else. When the patriarch of our family finally fell away, it was church people, the congregation, who surrounded us, comforted us, made the day-to-day functions of living a little more tolerable in a sea of grief. It was where baby showers were held for the preacher's daughter and for the daughter of the congregation who became pregnant out of wedlock. It was the parking lot where the turtle races were held during the summer festival.

I also never viewed guns as an "epidemic." They were what brought venison sausage to my family's table. They were what protected my life and the life of my family members one late-summer night as I slept in Grandma and Grandpa's bed. A mile away my aunt's estranged husband tried to kill her and threatened to follow her to my grandparents' house as she raced through the dark woods in nothing but a nightshirt to escape. It was the silhouette of my navy-veteran grandfather and his shotgun on the moonlit porch that ended the threat a full twenty minutes before the law arrived. Guns were what gave me safety and peace of mind while raising two babies in St. Louis when my neighbors and I discovered that a drug den had opened down the street.

The military is what one of my cousins admirably did after high school graduation, not some ridiculous topic of "imperialism" that hipster-suited coastals debate sans experience with authority at cocktail parties in our nation's capital. The summer before my sixth-grade year our family threw him a party on the riverbank, replete with a huge bonfire. Every night I watched the news about George H. W. Bush's campaign in

Iraq because it felt like we were tracking my cousin's movements on TV. My grandfather had been a gunner on the USS *Alabama* and with some prodding would tell fascinating tales about his time at sea. There isn't a family in Flyover Nation without military associations.

Caring for the environment is what my grandpa and family did every day, tending to cows, preventing overgrazing, growing crops, and controlling the predator population so that the population of each woodland denizen was at a healthy level. Mismanaging the land might mean your family went hungry for a season or you didn't have meat in your freezer. That's true conservation, not the religion of recycling preached by coastals who've never had to live off the land in the way that Flyover has for generations. People in Flyover develop a reverence for the land and wildlife in their care. Even now I can say without a doubt that southern Missouri is one of the most beautiful places on earth, if not *the* most beautiful. My childhood memories are of running through fields during the golden hour as the sun set, eating fresh watercress from the spring, catching tadpoles and crawfish in the Black River, going to bed with a belly full of venison and the smell of a wood fire in the air. You ask me to describe heaven and that's what I'd tell you. It's miles away from the freakish image coastal elites have concocted of Flyover.

When people in Flyover identify a problem, it's usually a problem they've seen up close. So we create workable solutions. What we consider problems and what coastal elites consider problems are vastly different things. I've noticed on the East and West Coasts, whenever a problem is identified the solution is always to appeal to government, and the more the solution costs, the better the solution. Not to mention that these solutions always include some limitation of the rights of others. A criminal illegally obtained and used a firearm to commit a crime? Certainly we must pass more restrictive gun laws for the law abiding to follow and the criminals to ignore! When the subject of gun homicide arises, the solution from the coasts is to always penalize the only people who actually go and get background checks and don't unlawfully carry. It never includes waging a campaign against the corrupt judge who reduced a felon's unlawful-carry gun charge to mere probation, which let him back on the street to reoffend, or disbarment of the judge who reduced a ten-year prison sentence for a straw purchaser to 180 days' house arrest. Increasing background checks on private, in-state transfers isn't going to impact criminal possession when criminals are barred from carrying anyway, much less purchasing. Not to mention that the message is contradictory: Everytown, a Michael Bloomberg–funded anti–Second Amendment group claims it's about saving kids, yet its political director, Matt Burgess, is also the political director for Planned Parenthood. Some reasoning Olympics must be involved to justify that contradiction. Perhaps the goal is to achieve fewer victims of gun violence by ensuring fewer of them make it out of the womb. But just "do something," they implore.

"Do something" isn't a slogan. It's a whine.

In Flyover it's believed criminals should be punished. On the East and West Coasts a doctrine of "rehabilitation" has taken root. Of course, they have to believe in it in order to reduce their out-of-control prison populations. Criminals thrive on such indulgence.

The East and West Coasts have difficulty reducing the abstraction of simple concepts like church, firearms, race relations/Black Lives Matter, conservation, ending rape culture, and Occupy Wall Street (OWS) to concrete, tangible solutions. A bunch of hippies camped out on Wall Street and defecated on cop cars. A lot of good that did anyone. What did they accomplish? Nothing. Black Lives Matter makes it a societal crime to suggest that all lives are equal and thus matter. They've demanded segregated spaces on college campuses, à la the sixties. What is the point? Third-wave feminists think it's a human rights issue that they have to pay for their own birth control pills, which explicitly concern sexual recreation. Every problem is always met as a civil rights issue, from hurt feelings to lack of participation trophies and the expectation that we live in a meritocracy. It's always met with some sort of protest where the same chants and slogans of the past fifty years are rehashed. Protests have turned into tantrums; coastals don't even know how to protest. The point of a protest is to bring awareness to a particular issue and use that momentum to effect actual, lasting change. OWS changed nothing, and Black Lives Matter only made it taboo to publicly state that every human is worthy of life, the opposite of the equality spirit its organizers claim motivates them. If left to the East and West Coasts, every problem would be met with government intervention and require much federal spending. In a materialistic culture, money thrown at problems is like fairy dust that makes it all better. The East and West Coasts don't like the market-directed minimum wage? Then petition the government to artificially increase the wages for menial labor, outpacing the pay of EMTs in certain areas, and increase the prices of the goods produced (goods mainly relied upon by those in lower income brackets) to justify them. Make said products more expensive so that the demand decreases and the business struggles to keep its doors open and employees on the payroll. Most of these pinkies-out, cocktail-drinking appletini fans selfishly entertain these grandiose plans of economic equality without realizing their negative impact on the very people they publicly pride themselves on helping. It's the true class warfare that's being ignored: the appropriation of middle-class struggles as a justification for implementing bigger government.

Coastal elites glom on to issues like the above just as they do branding. Using Apple products suggests something different from using a PC; claiming you're for certain issues brands you too, in an era where everything is all marketing and no soul. Meanwhile, in Flyover it's all soul and no marketing, which is why our values and ideas have been so underserved and underrepresented all these years. These are issues we know intimately. Coastals know about guns because they watched *The Matrix*; Flyover knows them because they got an NRA junior membership and a deer rifle as a gift for their thirteenth birthday. Coastal elites champion factory workers from Hollywood; Flyover knows them because their mom worked the night shift in a granola bar factory and one of the perks was trash bags of granola bars for each employee to bring home every Friday. For Flyover these are real issues, not just themes paraded on the Sunday talk show circuit; this is what Flyover wakes up to, lives with, and goes to sleep with each evening. It's hard to abstract and overanalyze what you live. It's not just a cultural difference; it's a difference in realities.

Imagine how different our politics would look if the DC smart set spent a little time out here in the real America with the hoi polloi. Imagine if just a few of them came next Sunday and sat in the pew with you.

CHAPTER 1

You Can't Unfriend Family

When I was a kid a giant poster of New York City hung in my room. It was a poster of the Brooklyn Bridge at night, the city lit up like the Fourth of July behind it and in the bottom right corner a dimly lit riverfront street I didn't know. The poster took up half the width of my bedroom wall at my home in southern Missouri. To me it represented everything my rural community south of St. Louis did not: excitement, adventure, opportunity, sophistication. Everything I knew about New York came from *The Baby-Sitters Club: Stacey's Mistake* (No. 18). I wanted to picnic in Central Park. I wanted to see the museums and eat lox and bagels. But when I visited Manhattan for the first time, my childhood dream was shattered, because no matter how large my poster was, it couldn't convey the size of the city. I felt like the buildings were long fingers clasping over me, and I couldn't see the wide-open sky. It was pointless to drive a car anywhere, and the first time I tried to relax in Central Park two homeless people fought in front of me and everywhere smelled like urine and pretzels. The childhood Dana took down that Brooklyn Bridge poster from her mind's bedroom wall.

I never realized my attachment to that wide-open Flyover sky until I had to do without it. As much as I wanted to love and fall in love with NYC, I couldn't. My very first visit to the city left me overwhelmed. I was in town to appear on Wendy Williams's television show. The staff was wonderful and gracious; they put me up at the W in midtown, and some band booked on Jimmy Fallon's late-night show played me to sleep in Times Square. There were so many people and so many things and advertisements and cars and noise that I went to Sbarro, got a slice of pizza, and holed up in my room for the rest of the day watching the city parade past, many stories up, through the glass. I got more adventurous with every visit, although my views of the city were mainly limited to what I could see through the tinted windows of a studio-hired car en route to this or that network. I've been to NYC more times than I can count at this point, but every time I go I take a big breath as the bridge dumps me out of Queens and into Manhattan. I also can't sleep without a white-noise machine that plays crickets and frogs.

My childhood was fraught with upheaval, a tempestuous childhood of domestic violence that resulted in a struggling single-parent household in Flyover. My mother worked in the city because the jobs were in the city, not in the rolling hills and green pastures of the rural farmland where she and the rest of my family originated and still live. I was angry at her for having us live so far from everyone we knew. I hated my elementary school and the kids who didn't like me: I was small for my age, reed thin, and unremarkable in every way. From my mother's feminist, leftist perspective, in rural America you were either a wife, a waitress, or a bank teller at the small branch in town—or you got lucky and scored a job as a makeup artist for the local mortician, as my mother's best friend did after high school. The city offered more opportunities for employment (for her) and education (for me). Every weekend we'd make the two-and-a-half hour journey back to "the country," as we simply called it, the nouveau city mice visiting the country mice. Every weekend my spirit was restored in a tiny one-room church, playing in the creek with my cousins, catching fireflies at dusk, and sleeping at the foot of my grandparents' woodstove as the sound of crickets lulled me to sleep; in the winter it was the sound of complete silence from the woods buried in snow. Nothing was ever so wonderful as being in the Ozarks. My cousins were cared for after school by my aunts, older cousins, and Grandmother. They grew up spending every day, not just weekends and summers, playing in the creek, picking corn, naming Grandpa's goats, chasing Grandma's pheasants when she wasn't looking. Their caregivers consisted of familiar places, familiar locations.

Everyone in the family knew where each grandkid was at any given point in the day. My cousins had one another at school during the day. If you messed with one, you messed with all. They attended one another's basketball and volleyball games; they cheered wildly whenever a cousin made a basket or scored a point. They rooted for one another at the town's annual beauty pageant and gathered at Grandma and Grandpa's beforehand to dress that year's appointed female cousin in the best gown and makeup the Ozarks had to offer. They attended church together and sat next to one another, filling up half the pews in the sanctuary. If you didn't have a father figure in your life there was Grandpa, a bevy of uncles, and older cousins there to fill the role. Everyone always had a partner at recess, company at dinner, a shoulder on which to cry, a hand to hold, a ride from school. They were separated from me by hours of asphalt and rolling hills.

In the city, no one knew who I was or to whom I belonged. An endless string of teenage girls babysat me after school. I felt no particular attachment to any of them. One time one of them forgot to make me lunch and instead made out with her boyfriend on my mom's bed. I turned up the television so *Heathcliff* would drown out their noises and then ran outside and down the steps to the sidewalk in front of our house, where I sat on the bottom step and embraced my knees. There was no one to whom I could run. I had no tribe. The neighbors on our left were a poor family whose daughter smoked pot and whose bedroom consisted of a mattress and rainbow curtains; her parents fought at night and I could hear her mother's every scream. The neighbors to our right were a family who seemed to find themselves in our hovelly hood due to hard times, and they kept to themselves. My mother did the best she could for me. I hid the transgressions of babysitters so that she wouldn't worry while she slaved away at one of the three jobs she worked so we could avoid taking government handouts.

No one knew me at school. I didn't fit in with the preps, the burnouts, the jocks; I didn't even fit in with the weirdos, which made me the weirdest weirdo of all. I ate lunch alone and pretended that people at my school who remotely looked like me were family members. I sat on the bus alone and no one noticed me. Literally. One day I forgot to get off at my stop and was too small for the driver to see. My mom and the school found me a couple of hours later, crying in my seat in the dark bus shed. It's amazing how you can feel lonelier in a city than in the country. In the city you're isolated by all of the nameless faces and the noise of their conversations. Everyone around you does what you do, so no one stands apart.

During recess I swung. It was a solo activity. I would swing higher and higher until I could look down the hill at the long drive that led up to my elementary school. I'd imagine my mom's green Oldsmobile coming up that windy drive to collect me early from school and take me away back down south to our family. Every Friday that's what she did: She picked me up after school and we'd escape. We'd eat sandwiches, or if I was lucky, I'd eat a McDonald's Happy Meal in the car. There wasn't time to stop and eat anywhere; Mom wanted to be on the road and get to the country as badly as I did. I'd hand her fries while she drove. We'd chase the last stretch of sunbeams across the plains until the white lines on the highway were all I could see. I'd drift off to sleep and wouldn't wake up until I could hear the crunch of Grandma and Grandpa's gravel drive under the well-worn tires of our thirdhand car.

Waking up on Saturday morning at Grandma and Grandpa's was magical. Sometimes I would be so tired that I'd sleep through the rooster's crow, but Grandma's bacon and eggs would wake me up every time. I'd get out of bed and make my way down the hall to their sun-drenched living room. I'd hug Grandpa first because he was always in his recliner, watching wrestling and drinking coffee.

"Are they treating you nice up there?" he'd always ask. I'd always answer yes, even if it wasn't true. I think he knew when it wasn't, but Grandpa never pried. He was selectively half deaf from firing .50 caliber guns on the USS *Alabama* during

World War II. He would pretend not to hear you when he didn't want to but always amazed us with what he would hear and inquire about later. After Grandpa, I'd find Grandma in the kitchen and hang on her waist while she fried eggs. My grandmother was a micromanaging matriarch with a terrible temper, but no one fiercely loved and protected their brood like this woman did. She would kiss my head and tell me that she'd made sure to fill the cookie jar before we arrived. Mom would sit at the kitchen table, smoking a cigarette while Grandma cooked. Mom would brief Grandma on everything during those Saturday mornings when I slept in: her divorce, her work, my school, how we were doing. After breakfast we dressed, and then by noon the entire family would descend on my grandparents' house. It was a Saturday tradition. The adults would visit and we kids would tear loose throughout the hills and valleys around Grandma and Grandpa's property.

Where I lived was very different from the country, where the Quik Mart owner, canoe rental proprietor, gas station attendant, town preacher, and everyone else recognized me without even hearing my family name, all because I had the family looks: dark hair, large dark eyes, olive skin, and a slender build.

"I know you. You're Gale's daughter," one would say. "You look just like all of 'em."

"Well, I'll be," said another. "You're the spittin' image of 'em all." They'd watch me and my cousins with amusement as we'd walk into the store barefoot, fresh from the creek, and pick up Sixlets and cream sodas before unfurling damp, wadded-up dollars on the counter to pay for them. There's a certain credit you carry when everyone knows your family. In the city your family name means nothing to anyone. Down here, down in these dark crevices of the Missouri hills, it means inclusion, belonging, familiarity, legacy. Family isn't perfect. You can't unfriend family; you can't unfollow them. They are yours. They are mine. And I know in my soul that if ever I found myself in a situation, my family would be there, just as I would be for them. My cousin once heard about threats I'd received and messaged me that he would "come to the city and sit on your porch with my shotgun." I cried for an hour straight. My Flyover family. They were bred for the woods, for the prairies, bred to live off nature, to fight, and to love. They live in one of the most beautiful parts of the United States, a place people don't see unless they look down from their plane windows at thirty thousand feet.

Aside from faith, name, looks, and mannerisms, I shared something else with my family: their politics. The stereotype is that country bumpkins are just one big Republican voting bloc. They've never met my family. I've said before that Bill Clinton was the second man after my father to screw me over, and it started me down a path of political self-discovery. My faith and my politics are intertwined because, you see, one led me to the other. It was my biggest vulnerability that drove me to God and to a deeper understanding of self-sustainability and responsibility.

I came from a broken home. I am a statistic in that regard. I had a horrible relationship with my father that followed me into my adulthood and nearly killed me spiritually. The entire first half of my life was tainted by its effect on me. I allowed it to control me. I hated men, I hated marriage, I never wanted children, and I believed that the only good place for a woman to be was on her own. I was rude to men, I was cruel to boys I dated, I was angry at the world, and I felt that the entire universe owed me a giant apology. I was uncomfortable in the homes of friends who had intact families. It didn't help that I had friends whose parents viewed me as damaged goods because I had a single mom at home. They went to big churches and prayed to God, but I didn't see any fruits of their faith in their hushed tones and condescending looks whenever my mother would collect me from their house in her old car. I resented them, I resented their faith, and I resented their wealth. I resented that they always had family in the stands cheering them on at track meets while it was rare for someone to be there for me. I raged at God in prayer.

Why did I get the shaft, God?! I would mentally scream. *Why did you do this to me? I thought you were omnipotent!* He just took it. He took all of it. Over the period of a few years He began to soften my heart (a child's heart!) to the point where I could open a Bible and read it. And I did. The first Bible I read was the giant Bible my grandma and grandpa kept on their coffee table. Some people keep art books or magazines on their coffee tables, but at my grandparents' house they kept a giant Bible. It was in a wooden box specially made for them by a cousin in shop class. Every now and then I saw Grandpa reading through it. (We later learned, after Grandpa got sick, that he hated banks and kept a sizable amount of money in his Bible. His reasoning was that "no heathen is going to take it.") I picked it up one weekend and spent an entire night reading the Gospels. That's how my journey began. I went to Sunday school and church with my grandma, aunts, and assorted cousins. It was a tiny little Baptist church in the hills with three rooms: one for worship and two classrooms for adults and kids in the basement. My family aren't what I'd call "holy rollers," but Grandpa would crack you with some Scripture when needed. It was from this that I asked my mom to start taking me to church. Mom picked up another job on certain weekends, so whenever she couldn't drive south she'd take me to church near our house. From there I attended church camp and was saved. The absence of a father figure in my life had created an abyss in my heart so deep that I almost couldn't function. Without even realizing what I was doing, I began seeking out a way to fill it and through this pain found my faith. I may not have had an earthly father, but I have a Father in heaven. I was saved at a country Baptist church camp when I was eleven. I am still growing in my faith to this day. It has not been without bumps along the way, particularly during my teenage years, but it has been my relationship with Christ alone that has brought me to where I am now.

It all began in my grandparents' living room with their coffee table Bible.

My family and other families in Flyover Nation have an odd tradition. For someone who dies in Flyover, popularity is measured in three ways: the number of flowers delivered to the funeral home for the wake/visitation, the length of the funeral procession, and the number of trinkets that cover a grave site in the years after someone dies.

An aunt of mine is family-famous for once encouraging family members to drive separate cars so it looked as though there were more people turning out for another family member's burial. When attending other visitations, it is not remarkable to see people taking inventory of who sent flowers and the sizes of the bouquets. If so-and-so sends Dorothy Smith's wake a big bouquet and sends someone else's only a peace lily—and so-and-so knows both in equal measure—there will be a cold war. Everyone knows that the peace lily is the lazy funeral flower. For instance, you do not send a peace lily to a close friend's or family member's visitation. It's the middle finger, the *I don't care* of funeral botanicals. If you don't send a family member visitation flowers for their loss, you might as well go and burn their house down and shoot their dog, such is the offense. The unwritten rule is that a person is on the hook for visitation flowers by twenty-one years of age. My mother once called *eleventy frillion* times in one week to make sure that I had ordered visitation flowers for Great-Great Aunt So-and-so (whom I could remember only for always having coral lipstick on her dentures), and *what time would they arrive?* My uncles had their own tradition, much to the funeral home owner's chagrin, of tucking a bottle of Busch beer between the body and the casket lining. In the town where my family originates, there is one undertaker and one funeral home. I always facetiously imagined him rubbing his hands together and counting his money as he watched the families in town gray and wither.

This flower business may sound wasteful, but where I'm from you want to live a good and generous life and you want everyone to know you were loved and respected for it. By "everyone" we mean everyone whose life you personally touched. Of no importance is how big the paper ran your obituary or whether anyone famous attended your funeral. Even though we believe our dearly departed have moved on to a better place, funerals are always heavy, somber, and emotional events. In certain parts of Flyover they serve double duty as family reunions, revivals, and theatrical performances, particularly in my family. It used to embarrass me, but in hindsight I view it as an extraordinary, unique quality of my family (but not to the point where I can't wait for the next death to witness it again). I hesitated for a bit to introduce my husband to my family. I had just turned twenty-one and we were engaged. My family was overjoyed simply because they had thought that either I was a lesbian or no man would take on the challenge of marrying me. When they got wind of Chris, my grandma said her prayers had been answered and one of my particularly frisky and liquoriffic aunts immediately asked when I was going to bring him down to meet all the kin. Unfortunately, before all of this was to happen my great-uncle, who lived in St. Louis, died. It was the rare relative who lived in the city, so the entire family was making the trek from down south to up north. I told Chris that I would see him later that weekend, as my family would be arriving soon and I needed to attend the visitation and funeral.

"Well, I am going too," he said.

"Oh, no, you're not," I replied.

"Oh, yes, I am," he countered. "You're my fiancée. I want to be there for you and your family." His poor, sweet little heart had no idea what it was asking. After some back-and-forth I conceded and resolved myself to being single after he met my family—at a visitation—for the first time. I coached him before the Friday-evening visitation.

"First," I instructed sharply, "do not make eye contact with any wailing people. If someone falls, step over them."

"If someone falls . . . ?"

"Step over them."

He was incredulous.

The day arrived and my family piled into the small sanctuary at the funeral home in the city. Most of them had crammed themselves into as few cars as possible, as all my aunts were terrified of driving anywhere beyond the reaches of southern

Missouri. Then my grandmother arrived. Most of the women in the family have always taken their lead from Grandma. If Oscars were awarded for performances not given on screen, the woman would be the most awarded thespian in all of the craft. Sometimes it was genuine emotion, but mostly she just liked the attention. I heard her sobbing before she even entered the room. She walked past, hanging on the arm of a second cousin, and made her way up to my great-uncle's casket.

Then the wailing began.

Grandma threw herself on the casket and screamed, "Why, God, why?"

"Because he was old and unwell?" I offered under my breath. An uncle elbowed me. Chris was stunned.

Other family members joined the Wailing. That was the signal to me, my cousins, and most of the men in the room to exit. Chris was on my arm and we made our way to the exit, which, unfortunately, was by the casket and the Wailing.

Chris was so close.

Just as we were at the home stretch, Grandma cast a cursory glance around the room before crumpling to the floor. I stepped around her. Chris did not. He was suckered. In the safety of the foyer our group of escapees took inventory of our numbers.

"Oh no . . ." I said softly.

"What is it?" asked a cousin.

"Chris. He stopped . . . he stopped to pick her up."

"Newbie," said an uncle as the rest murmured in agreement. About fifteen minutes later Grandma was escorted through the door clutching Chris's arm. She shot me a baleful look as she passed while Chris looked concerned but horrified.

"Well, she got him," said another cousin. I thought for sure he'd ask for the ring back in the parking lot.

"I won't judge you until you come to one of my family reunions," he said before hugging me.

In my family's town there is a process for death. Oftentimes family will elect to have home hospice, as in the case of my grandmother, and have the family member pass at home. Home births, why not home deaths? The family preacher comes to visit, often bringing a handkerchief with which to wipe his brow after a furious prayer session. Family gathers, food is delivered, and everyone pretends that they're not just staring and watching for the death mask.

What I experienced at visitations and funerals growing up couldn't have been more different from the restrained sophistication of such events that I attended on the coasts. I read an article recently where the author lamented the loss of the funeral. In place of mourning, families were instead opting for "celebrations of life." We once attended a friend's funeral on the West Coast, where we saw this phenomenon. People celebrated in lieu of mourning. It struck me as odd. I felt out of place holding a champagne glass and laughing next to a posterized 11×17 of the departed. Everyone was dressed fabulously and it felt like Fashion Week. I added up seventeen thousand dollars' worth of Louboutins on the feet of the women chatting while waiting at the bar. It felt like it would be a fashion faux pas if anyone were to cry. Another such event on the East Coast felt similar. It was billed as a "celebration of life" of the departed. The funeral service pared down any religiousliciousness and opted for one anemic prayer. There was no graveside service; instead the cavalcade of black BMWs, Mercedes, and Volvos made its way to an Italian restaurant that was rented out for

21

the life celebration. The widow was on uppers so as not to fall apart in front of guests. Isn't that when you *should* fall apart? While friends and family are there to uplift you? I didn't understand—and frankly was beyond embarrassed by—my own family's funeral theatrics until I experienced some of the emotion-choking formats of life celebrations. No one wants to be happy and all the smiles are fake.

My family may fall to the floor and bawl like toddlers denied a toy at Walmart, but they get it all out of their system.

When I die, I don't want a celebration. I want people to be *sad* because *something sad happened*. I don't want to have a such a tenuous connection to people in my life that they'll attend my funeral only if it looks like it's going to be fun. I don't want the loss of life to be a *party* because it's not. I want people to attend because they feel a moral obligation to pay respects to my loved ones and to share fellowship with one another, to honor the moral bond that linked us in life. From my experiences in Flyover Nation, a funeral isn't just some posthumously hosted celebration; it's a way for people to honor the purpose of life and the effect that this life in particular had on others. A funeral in Flyover is a also religious observance that recognizes God's design, culminating in the end of life. There is a certain joy, to be sure, the joy we feel is knowing that we will see our loved one again because of our relationship with God through Christ Jesus. Chad Bird, in the *Federalist*, summarizes these "end of life celebrations":

> *The danger is simply this: that we downplay death and, in so doing, fail to fully appreciate life Stripped of its euphemistic language, the get-together billed as a "celebration" or even a "party" is, in truth, a gathering of*

mourners around a corpse. And that dead body not only preaches that death has claimed this particular life, but it betokens our own inevitable demise. To the extent that we bury our head in the sand when confronted with the reality of death, to that same extent we miss out on an opportunity to learn more about, and to appreciate more deeply, the life that is ours. It should come as no surprise that a culture which has euphemized the beginning of life has also euphemized its end.[1]

Birth can be predicted; death, in most cases, cannot. In our world the body is a containment unit for the soul. The body is a vessel through which we experience the joys and horrors of this imperfect world, like a virtual-reality experience. When we use up our shell, we discard it in plots that perforate the earth or we burn to dust. Either way, I've never felt celebratory looking at an empty body in a casket. The first funeral I ever attended was that of a junior high school classmate who drowned in a lake one fall. I huddled with my friends by the casket and stared at his smooth, artificially peach skin. He looked as though he could wake up at any moment. Since then I've witnessed the burial of grandparents, aunts, and uncles. I've watched as the older generation of my family has rotated into heaven, thereby placing my generation—myself and cousins, we "grandkids"— a step up in both hierarchy and distance from death.

Perhaps one of the oddest traditions my family observes, and I'm not even certain this is unique to my family or other families in Flyover (a friend from Kansas admitted that her family did the same thing), is that of the graveyard vigil. I have nothing else to call it, but that's exactly what it is. My family members regularly visited our departed at the family cemetery

atop a hill overlooking an Ozark valley. The view is breath-
taking, and I often wondered why the property was wasted on
people who would never see it.

"So the living visiting their relatives can enjoy it," snapped
Mom once during one such "vigil" visit. She was frustrated at
having to move around all the gewgaws that littered my grandparents' tombstones to the point where the names were no longer visible. My uncle was in his farm overalls and had brought
with him a giant trash bag into which he swept all the trinkets
with several motions of his arm. It was my last visit to the family cemetery there in the Ozarks, and we went with my aunt
and uncle, my mother's brother and sister. You could see which
graves were my grandparents' upon arrival, as they were the
only ones with their own flagpole, wind chimes, and assortment of fiber-optic angels. I had no idea who thought that wind
chimes made sense in a graveyard, but there they were, ringing
with the breeze above the granite markers. The fiber-optic
angels were even weirder. Apparently Grandma liked them, or
someone in the family had decided she did. I personally thought
they were bizarre because all of their faces were so cheaply
painted so that they looked like *The Dark Crystal* characters.
During her dying days, my aunts and uncles set up her deathbed in the living room of their tiny country home, and at the
foot of her bed one of my aunts arranged a small army of fiber-
optic angels to comfort her. Grandma was on morphine so she
was high as a kite, and I can't imagine what it looked like in her
mind every time she opened her eyes and saw a mob of dis-
torted faces with creepy, disproportionate arms, skinny fingers,
and ever-changing rainbow-colored wings reaching out to her
from the foot of her bed.

"I promise to never get you a fiber-optic angel," I told my

mother as she helped my uncle bag up the trinkets so she could lay flowers on the graves.

Hospice helped care for Grandma and when her time was close, the family called Brother Jim, the family preacher, to the house to pray over her. She refused to die while people were in the room. As macabre as it sounds, I found this humorous, as it was a testament to the woman's sheer strength of will and vanity. Her *entire* body would shut down, but if Grandma Boots wasn't ready to die yet, well, there would be no dyin', and Grandma wasn't going to die in *front* of people. Grandma didn't like wearing her pajamas in front of people or having her short, Elvis'd Nice'n Easy Black No. 1 hair messy if someone called. She also didn't drive, as she preferred to be *driven*.

So it made sense that Grandma tried to die one night when Mom stayed over and fell asleep in the recliner next to her bed. According to Mom, she opened her eyes right as the "death mask" flashed across Grandma's face, and when Mom yelled out in fright, Grandma stopped. After that I think Mom tried to stay up to stare all night at her, but a couple of days later the family realized that they needed to give Grandma some quiet time to see what happened. Otherwise who knew how long the woman would hang on in spite of the laws of nature? One afternoon they did just that, giving Grandma her space. Grandma finally sensed that she had the privacy she wanted and deserved and chose that moment to answer the call and return home to Jesus.

Where my family is from "euthanasia" means putting a cow or horse out of its misery after it fatally injures itself. Applied to a person it is defined as murder. They would never think of robbing God of a scene from His master plan. As difficult as our exits may sometimes be, they serve a purpose. Things are seen quite differently on the coasts.

California's state legislature legalized physician-assisted suicide in a bill signed by Governor Jerry Brown. It made California the fifth state, along with Washington, Oregon, Montana, and Vermont, to allow physician-assisted suicide. Other states have proposed such legislation but no others have yet passed it. The movement got its face with the death of Brittany Maynard, who had terminal brain cancer and moved from California to Oregon to end her life. She was a beautiful young woman who was devoted to education and traveled the world. She killed herself on November 1, 2014. She wrote in an article for CNN:

> *I've had the medication for weeks. I am not suicidal. If I were, I would have consumed that medication long ago. I do not want to die. But I am dying. And I want to die on my own terms. I would not tell anyone else that he or she should choose death with dignity. My question is: Who has the right to tell me that I don't deserve this choice? That I deserve to suffer for weeks or months in tremendous amounts of physical and emotional pain? Why should anyone have the right to make that choice for me?*[2]

I can completely understand that choice if you think your life is your own. That's not what most in Flyover believe, or most Christians, for that matter. Our lives are not our own. That choice is made already. God is not ambiguous in the Bible when He condemns the taking of innocent life.

Maynard's story was aided by groups like Death with Dignity, also the common phrase used when describing legalized suicide. The phrase itself is insulting, as though those who've died by any other means did so without dignity—or those who choose to allow God to determine how their lives end are somehow undignified in their choice.

Death on demand is now a lifestyle in Holland and other parts of the Netherlands. It has become such an issue that eighty well-known and respected Brits—including Hugh Grant, Eric Idle, Patrick Stewart, and an assortment of lords and ladies— wrote letters to the *Telegraph* demanding an examination of the issue before Parliament, writing:

> *Most people in Britain support law change on assisted dying, and no one believes that someone should face a prison sentence of 14 years for compassionately assisting a loved one to die. We are closer than ever to allowing dying people to have safeguarded choice in how they approach their deaths. Whoever forms the next government must allow time for Parliament to reach consensus on a safeguarded law.*[3]

In Flyover the only legitimate death assistance anyone requires is for the jailer to pull the lever and execute a criminal whose punishment was justifiably worthy of capital punishment. Physician-assisted suicide is a glossy term for euthanasia or, more plainly, a very late-term abortion. It's the ending of a life due to inconvenience. Circumstances, not God, determine viability, and our culture is marching ever toward vesting an immoral, godless government with the power to determine both circumstance *and* viability. There is no such thing as a slippery-slope fallacy when discussing the abuse of regulatory powers by the government. It's simply an observation of statistics. Soon people will argue that physician-assisted suicide promotes inequality, as those of lesser means may lack the ability to pay for an assist. Don't roll your eyes: We subsidize infanticide as birth control in clinics that are allowed to skirt the medical standards other actual health-care clinics are required to meet. Euthanasia is the devolution of medicine. It's a lazy escape for medical professionals who confuse surrender with compassion. Holland legalized euthanasia years ago and is described as "out of control" by doctors. From the *Daily Mail*:

The number of mentally-ill patients killed by euthanasia in Holland has trebled in the space of a year, new figures have revealed. In 2013, a total of 42 people with "severe psychiatric problems" were killed by lethal injection compared with 14 in 2012 and 13 in 2011. The latest official figures also revealed a 15 per cent surge in the number of euthanasia deaths from 4,188 cases in 2012 to 4,829 cases last year.

[. . .]

The rise is also likely to confirm the fears of Dutch regulator Theo Boer who told the Daily Mail that he expected to see euthanasia cases smash the 6,000 barrier in 2014. Overall, deaths by euthanasia, which officially account for three per cent of all deaths in the Netherlands, have increased by 151 per cent in just seven years.

[. . .]

The figures, however, do not include cases of so-called terminal sedation, where patients are given a cocktail of sedatives and narcotics before food and fluids are withdrawn.

*Studies suggest that if such deaths were added to the
figure then euthanasia would account for one in eight—
about 12.3 per cent—of all deaths in the Netherlands.
Dr Peter Saunders of the Christian Medical Fellowship
said the Dutch experiment proved that doctor-assisted
death was impossible to effectively regulate.*

*"Euthanasia in the Netherlands is way out of con-
trol," he said.*

In 2013 Holland "euthanized" 650 babies, as reported by
the *Daily Mail:*[4]

*But the euthanasia business does not just concern the
elderly. It is now acceptable for a doctor to end the life
of a baby, with the parents' consent, if it is in pain or
facing a life of hopeless suffering. The Royal Dutch
Medical Association estimates that 650 newborns are
killed every year because they fall into this category.*[5]

It is also a safety precaution for the innocent: Life falls under
God's domain, not man's.

There isn't a lack of dignity in pain or in having family care
for you as you die. We don't dictate the terms of our birth and
have little more control over our death.

You can see this selfishness coming through in the debate over
abortion, as well. The coastal approach has always been that a
pregnancy is nobody else's business, especially excluding consideration of the life in the womb.

Do abortion advocates know how babies are made? I ask

because they always act so surprised if intercourse results in pregnancy. One doesn't "accidentally" become pregnant. It's not as though you can walk down the sidewalk, trip, and—ta-da!—you're pregnant. You don't fall down and in the process of falling lose your clothes and land in bed with a member of the opposite sex. Even with most birth control methods on the market today, there is no such thing as "pregnancy proof." The choice comes *before* conception. Every time you have sex, unless you're elderly, have had a hysterectomy, or are infertile due to another issue, you risk creating new life. This is how science works. The amazing thing about science is that, coupled with capitalism, it's allowed for numerous women's choices before conception. You can purchase birth control for a few bucks a month at your local Target, Costco, etc. I realize that Sandra Fluke requested thousands of dollars a year in free birth control—which for that price must be some Louis Vuitton birth control talon rolled in fourteen-karat-gold flakes by bald eagles—but for us plebes you can get it for a fraction of that cost. Republicans even introduced legislation to make birth control available over the counter, but for some reason the Official Party for Women's Health and Victimization® opposes it and has blocked it from the floor for quite some time. Planned UnParenthood also opposes it, as it would cut into their revenue. We can't give women the ability to walk into a pharmacy and buy inexpensive, over-the-counter birth control on their own! Why, that would bite into Cecile Richards's Lamborghini money! Videos released in 2015 by the watchdog journalism site Center for Medical Progress caught numerous top docs and staffers with Planned Parenthood discussing how they sell infant body parts for profit. Using cagey language, they mentioned how they keep affiliates happy by watching "their bottom line," which suggests that the money received does more than pay for shipping and processing costs, as originally defended by Cecile Richards. The videos shocked those who live in a pretend world where infants are removed from the womb using magic instead of scissors, forceps, and vacuums. Richards later released a statement saying that Planned Parenthood would no longer charge companies like Stem Express for aborted infant body parts, destroying their earlier denial that such sales even took place. Over the 2015 Thanksgiving weekend a nut named Robert Lewis Dear engaged in a shootout with cops that reportedly began outside but involved a Colorado Springs Planned Parenthood facility when Dear holed up inside. Planned Parenthood wasted no time in fundraising off the attacks, pushing the narrative that Dear "targeted" the clinic (eyewitness accounts had placed the start of the incident at a nearby Chase Bank) and demanding that Republicans denounce Dear even though he wasn't a Republican or involved with any pro-life group. Murder is wrong, be it what Dear did or what abortionists inside Planned Parenthood clinics do every day, but you solve it with the justice system, not reckless, murderous vigilantism.

According to its own figures available on its Web site, Planned Parenthood makes the vast majority of its bank off abortions, yet it pushes the narrative that it offers women's health services, as though that evens out its practices. In reality, health services offered by Planned Parenthood have *decreased* over the years as its focus has sharpened on abortion. Meanwhile, community health centers far outnumber (three to one) Planned Parenthood facilities in every single state and offer exponentially more services for women. In addition, they meet the same standards required by states for medical clinics, a requirement Planned Parenthood unsuccessfully fought in Texas. Wendy Davis tried making her name off this fight, which occurred when lawmakers in Texas introduced legislation requiring Planned Parenthood facilities to meet greater standards of care for women. The law was proposed in the wake of infamous serial killer abortionist Kermit Gosnell, whose award-winning work (yes, really) at his Philadelphia clinic was called into question when his facility was raided in 2010 by the DEA on suspicion of illegal prescription drug practices. Agents discovered a house of horrors: a filthy facility, untrained workers performing procedures, babies shoved into shoe boxes and stored in freezers. The raid resulted in eight murder charges (among others) and a life sentence for Gosnell. Jurors heard of botched procedures that resulted in death, patients restrained and their infants aborted *after* they changed their minds, and other horrors. I read the grand jury report and cried. Sadly, this isn't an exception in this industry; it seems like the rule.

When the Planned Parenthood bill was introduced in the Texas legislature, Davis and infanticide advocates fought to stop it, massing in Austin and protesting wildly, including screaming "Hail Satan" on video and throwing used tampons, jars of urine, and feces.[6] The bill simply increased standards of care for women patronizing Planned Parenthood's Texas facilities and required, among other commonsense measures, that abortionists have admitting privileges at local hospitals. Proving that it's "all about women's care," Planned Parenthood opposed increasing its standards of care and threatened instead to shut down its clinics and blame Texas lawmakers, falsely stating that *Texas* was going to close clinics when, in fact, it was Planned Parenthood's infantile decision. The so-called champion of women's health wasn't an equal champion of its intellect.

Planned Parenthood fights against women's choice by falsely presenting to them a limited number of choices. It lied about providing mammograms—not just referrals, which don't constitute a service, but *actual* mammograms—and refuses to acknowledge that there exist better and more clinics that offer more services and better standards of care and serve more people than Planned Parenthood. But doing so wouldn't be great for its "bottom line."

Sometimes, when a media outlet sends a reporter out to visit the heartland to see what we're up to, they'll stumble upon the supposed irony that many of the states with the highest numbers of unplanned pregnancies are pro-life and in the South or Midwest. That's a backward way of thinking about it. The truth of the matter is that in states where we spend more time interacting with real people dealing with these issues, we tend to come out pro-life. It's much easier to support abortion rights when you don't have to actually think about someone you know killing their unborn child.

When I was pregnant with my firstborn, I was friends with a woman who was also expecting. She was one month ahead of me. I stopped speaking to her after she told me she was going to abort her child because she and her husband already had a toddler and couldn't afford a second child. Her husband didn't work, yet the solution to their situation wasn't for him to get a job; it was for them to murder their baby. I tried talking her out of it but it was hopeless. Her heart was hardened and her mind made up. Abortions are rare in my family's town. It's more shameful to abort an unplanned pregnancy than to become pregnant unplanned. People in Flyover believe in redemption and grace, because we've all needed it. Single motherhood and teenage motherhood aren't encouraged, but when they happen, it is done, and people focus on raising a baby rather than on blame. When a cousin of mine fell pregnant out of wedlock with no hope of the baby's father taking part, the family rallied, hosting a baby shower, purchasing all of the clothes for the first year, diapers, even gift cards to be used at the grocery store. One thing about Flyover: No one raises a baby here totally alone.

CHAPTER 2

Against the Powers of This Dark World

My parents divorced when I was very young, and for a lot of my life it was just me and my mother. I have no relationship now with my biological father. Long ago he joined my Internet trolls and for a time enjoyed crudely abusing me on Facebook and in comments sections of Web sites. He once wrote to a progressive blogger explaining that he was a hardcore Democrat and that I, a conservative, had lost my way, as though name-dropping a daughter he hadn't seen in over a decade gave him some sort of insider information. (The blogger, while disagreeing with me on most everything, kindly forwarded to me the correspondence.) He once even called an affiliate radio station and threatened to sue them if I ever mentioned him in a negative light on air. Amazingly, his aggressive behavior toward me had nothing to do with my conservative conversion, so absent was he in my life. That I came from a broken home did affect me, though in an opposite way from what progressives might think. It served to fuel my early progressive politics. I was let down in the most egregious way by a parent, a man. This created a chip on my shoulder that wasn't buffed out until my midtwenties. It started me on the path toward feminism. I never wanted to be dependent on a member of the opposite sex for any emotional, financial, or physical security. Oddly, the more feminist I became, the more I began to see that this was quite the opposite of the aim of the third-wave movement. (More on that to come.) I decided early on that if I *was* to marry, it would be for no other reason than that I was more certain of my potential union than I was of my next breath. I married when I was twenty-one years old and celebrated my fifteenth wedding anniversary this year. I am in my thirties now, and what I've learned is that marriage isn't a sprint; it's a marathon. It's love and work. It's patience. It's at odds with our instant-gratification society, which teaches the idiotic concept of "starter marriages" (like a starter house, but for your love life) and sanctions emotional adultery. I am harsh on divorce. I am harsh on people who take their spouses for granted, stop courting, stop loving, and ruin their families. I watched, heartbroken, as the marriages of two of our friends dissolved because of pure, unadulterated selfishness. I cannot take seriously the protests of any postured Christian who commits marital seppuku with dishonesty and adultery while pointing fingers at gay America for ruining marriage. No, you did a fine job of that yourself.

The majority of Americans (around seven in ten)[7] identify as Christian, to be sure. America is still home to more Christians than anywhere else in the world; at least, that's the statistic thrown out whenever people of faith decry the recent uptick in stateside religious persecution. Believing in God is one thing; believing in Jesus, becoming a *disciple*, not just a follower, fellowshipping regularly by attending church, that's something entirely different. Many put on their faith along with their Sunday best, true, and some posture to shepherd the faith with questionable doctrine that widens the gap between people and God. Society doesn't make it easy. If you watch television, go to the movies, or in any way participate in pop culture, you'd think that Christians were the minority. In culture, church and faith are sidelined.

There must be something about church that coastals really want to push out of the mainstream.

The town my family is from is made up of 301 people, at the last census. It includes a restaurant called, literally, "The Rest'urnt," a gas station and convenience mart, a small bank, and three churches that all exist within sight of one another: the Baptist church, the Church of the Nazarene, and Happy Zion Church. They're all salt-of-the-earth people. Amusingly, the Church of the Nazarene made a couple of townsfolk upset (or jealous) by building a ginormous new building that looks like a slightly uneven cross from above. My uncle Junior leads the church choir at the Baptist church. Uncle Junior is the 1970s manifest in one man. An upstanding man of God, he's tall and southern proper, he prefers brown polyester leisure suits and gold aviators, he wears a gold pinkie ring, and he coifs his black hair back behind his ears. If everyone has a personal theme song,

Uncle Junior's is Ram Jam's "Black Betty," and his stride matches the beat. During Sunday-morning services Uncle Junior Ram Jam–walks into the sanctuary, adjusting the robe over his shoulders as he snaps the choir to attention. The church organist lays her hands on the keys at the jab of his finger, and we're off to worship, spilling a week's worth of trials from our lungs in praise as the organist loses herself in the music, the flourishes, the theatrics before the keys, driving the hymn within an inch of sin with emotional, musical passion. It should be noted that no one actually knows Uncle Junior's real first name, except perhaps for his dearly departed wife, my great-aunt W. Many of the people from my family's town are known by nicknames only—Speedy, Too Tall (a cousin, reportedly), Clunker, Boots, etc.—and for a spell were even listed in the official town phone book in the same manner. It is, in every respect, a stereotypical country town in Flyover Nation, similar to Walkerton, Indiana, except perhaps Walkerton is a lot bigger with its fancy McDonald's and Main Street storefronts.

Walkerton is a thirty-minute drive south of South Bend, Indiana. It was this town that a reporter named Alyssa Marino from ABC 57 visited in search of content for a story on the state's new Religious Freedom Restoration Act. Business rights were in the news, with a string of bakers, photographers, and T-shirt makers in court citing faith as the reason why they wouldn't cater, make a cake for, make a T-shirt for, or photograph a same-sex marriage ceremony. Marino went to Flyover Nation in search of a stereotypical Christian business owner to answer on record whether or not they'd serve same-sex couples. She found a small-town pizza joint in Walkerton, with crosses on the walls, called Memories Pizza. It was to this business, specifically daughter Crystal O'Connor, who was manning the register that day, that Marino asked her question: Would the pizza parlor cater a gay wedding? Let it settle in, the insane context of this question and where it was asked. The Lois Lane of gay wedding journalism, Alyssa Marino, asked a small-town pizza parlor whether or not it would cater a gay wedding. Has Marino ever *met* a gay person? I have gay friends and family members. Not a single one of them would ever cater their wedding with *pizza*. My gay neighbors in our old neighborhood held a block party once and had *bottle service*. I'm from the Ozarks, and while I've had kin who disassembled and stored their Harleys in their living rooms during winter (sensible), not a single one of them would cater a wedding with pizza. I was disappointed that Marino asked only a hypothetical question and didn't bring along any actual gay customers as props to get an *actual* refusal of service on camera, Oprah style, but this is a reporter who *went to a small-town pizza joint to ask about catering a wedding*. I was shocked Marino didn't follow up by visiting a QuikTrip and asking if it would do the same. All O'Connor said was that Memories Pizza would, in fact, serve gay customers. The owners just didn't want to cater a gay wedding, declining to participate in an activity that didn't jibe with their sincere faith.

I mulled two motivations as the Internet batted about this rage ball like catnipped kitties: Either Marino is the dull, nubbin-tipped crayon in a box of new, perfectly sharpened Crayolas or she knew people wouldn't pay attention enough to notice that hers was a hypothetical question and that no service was actually refused—but the truth would be irrelevant, as people with agendas would conflate the two anyway. Ignoring this, Marino proved with her skill set why she works in a smaller, local market; her disingenuously ridiculous headline, which was quickly altered[8] after blowback, was RFRA: FIRST BUSINESS TO PUBLICLY DENY SAME SEX SERVICE. No. O'Connor did not "deny same sex service," nor did O'Connor say she would "deny same sex service," publicly or otherwise. What was specifically said was that the parlor would not *participate* in the activity of *catering a same-sex wedding*. I realize this obvious distinction is lost on people like Marino, who likely couldn't spell "nuance" without the benefit of spell-check, but alas, it's an important difference. The Internet Rage Mob® didn't care. They wanted blood; they protest for the pure carnage of silencing any and all opposition. Death of diverse thought by a million paper cuts.

They didn't get it.

Yes, the O'Connors had to temporarily close up shop and hide out in their home with the blinds closed, and yes, they even prepared to shutter the business entirely and leave the state.

But Flyover Nation flexed its muscles.

I'd had it. This was the modus operandi of the secular left: isolate, boycott, and destroy. These viral, rage-addicted vampires are always more concerned with how they're going to look to strangers on Tumblr or Instagram than with what happens to people in real life. This is what happens to people when they lose their sense of community.

After watching them successfully do it to a number of businesses and individuals, I knew they had to be stopped, and stopped in a magnificent, narrative-destroying manner. Enraged at this snuffing out of diverse thought, my *Blaze* staff and I created a fund-raising campaign for the pizza shop–owning O'Connors to help offset the cost of lost business. I covered it on my radio and television programs. I pushed it on social media. Flyover denizens responded by raising nearly a million dollars for Memories Pizza. It was one of the largest fund-raisers in GoFundMe's history, but the site wouldn't acknowledge it for fear of retribution from the "tolerant" secular Left. I didn't care. *They knew.* We knew. *Everyone knew.* That they couldn't bring themselves to even acknowledge it out of hateful spite was further proof of victory. I could have continued. We could have raised over a million. Memories Pizza became a lightning rod, the second exception in this ongoing issue to the Alinsky tactics of isolate and destroy. The first was Chick-fil-A.

A few years ago the East and West Coasts, along with the Left's viral vampires spread throughout the Twittersphere, suddenly realized Chick-fil-A was a Christian-owned establishment. Never before had chicken sandwiches so roiled a country. The Left decided that they couldn't just order a chicken sandwich without first subjecting the seller to a litmus test on same-sex marriage. It sounds like a *Portlandia* episode. Chick-fil-A CEO Dan Cathy responded to the *Baptist Press* in an interview that he was "guilty as charged" in support of traditional marriage. Cathy told the outlet:

> *We are very much supportive of the family—the biblical definition of the family unit. We are a family-owned business, a family-led business, and we are married to our first wives. We give God thanks for that.*
>
> *We operate as a family business. . . . Our restaurants are typically led by families; some are single. We want to do anything we possibly can to strengthen families. We are very much committed to that.*

We intend to stay the course. We know that it might not be popular with everyone, but thank the Lord, we live in a country where we can share our values and operate on biblical principles.[9]

Secularists, who'd likely never read the *Baptist Press*, lost their ever-loving minds. They staged boycotts, sit-ins, and kiss-ins and vowed to shut down the fast-food chain. Chicago mayor Rahm Emanuel famously said, "Chick-fil-A values are not Chicago values." Yes, because selling chicken sandwiches is incompatible with the gangbanging, drug-pushing Chicago way of life, apparently.

The Chick-fil-A protest backfired, setting a sales record as Christians (and really, just sensible people who love good fried chicken and indoor playgrounds) flocked to their nearest outlet in the midst of the frenzy.

Progressives targeted also the Robertson family and *Duck Dynasty* after patriarch Phil Robertson spoke in favor of traditional marriage. The entire family stuck together, claiming that if Phil went, so too would they—and A&E's biggest cash-cow television series to date. Robertson was absent a few episodes but returned, and the family continued. So strong is their popularity that they've branched into retail with products ranging from Miss Kay's kitchens to brother Jep's beard balm (not to mention a few best-selling books).

The Benham brothers, twins David and Jason, were to host an HGTV program called *Flip It Forward*, until progressive Web sites pressed for the duo's cancellation because they are Christian and support traditional marriage. I appeared on television to discuss the story and listened as progressives who have done less for their fellow man than the Benhams accuse the twins of bigotry because they follow Scripture. The campaign against them was an anti-Christian smear campaign.

Most of the time, however, the viral vampires go after small targets with fewer ways to defend themselves.

They're not attacking an illegal activity, but they are trying to make holding an opinion different from their own an illegal act.

A Lexington, Kentucky, T-shirt shop called Hands On Originals was found in violation of "antidiscrimination" laws because the owner, a devout Christian, declined to print T-shirts for a gay-pride event.[10]

Hands On Originals and its owner, Blaine Adamson, said they declined the 2012 T-shirt order because of religious beliefs and disagreed with the shirt's message, which included the words "Lexington Pride Festival" with a list of sponsors of the gay-pride event on the back.

Adamson even suggested other T-shirt printers with comparable prices, but the organization behind the event wanted *Adamson's* shop, and in protest of being denied exercise of their belief in commerce, they succeeded in infringing on Adamson's beliefs. Surely Adamson's shop wasn't the only T-shirt shop in or near Lexington; a quick search turned up several printing shops in Lexington proper, and even more just on the outskirts.

New Mexico photographer Elaine Huguenin was targeted by a lesbian couple, Vanessa Willock and Misti Collinsworth, who apparently believed that Huguenin was the only wedding photographer in all of the state. Willock inquired about Huguenin's services for a "same gender ceremony," to which Huguenin replied that she only photographed "traditional weddings." Willock and Collinsworth immediately sued, citing discrimination. The couple wanted the State of New Mexico to compel Huguenin to use her talent—her free expression—as they saw fit without any regard for whether the content of that required expression conflicted with Huguenin's own personal beliefs. So far the State of New Mexico has won against Huguenot in court, thereby establishing the precedent that artists have no freedom to accept or decline commissioned work.

A same-sex couple from California sued a Hawaiian bed-and-breakfast privately owned by a Christian woman because she declined them a room due to her devout beliefs.[11] A number of bed-and-breakfasts from Hawaii to Vermont have faced this same fight. In January 2012 a judge ruled against a *church* in New Jersey[12] that declined use of its own property for a same-sex wedding. Catholic Charities was barred from assisting in adoptions in Massachusetts, Washington, DC, and Illinois and excluded from future contracts because it declined to consider same-sex couples.

Sweet Cakes, a bakery run by Melissa Klein, an Oregon baker and mother of five, was maliciously and ruthlessly targeted by the gay brigade for declining to bake a wedding cake for a same-sex couple. Rachel and Laurel Bowman-Cryer sued Aaron and Melissa Klein, forcing the bakery to close its doors (remodeled on a modest budget by Melissa when she excitedly opened her first storefront), and won damages of $75,000 and $60,000 for Laurel and Rachel, respectively, which will bankrupt the family. That's $135,000 for a *cake*. To receive this money, the Bowman-Cryers claimed they felt "mentally raped" in a list of eighty-eight symptoms of emotional distress at being refused a cake:

In January 2015, an investigation by the bureau found the Kleins guilty of violating the state's public accommodation law by denying Rachel and Laurel full and equal access to their bakery, which the state considers a place of public accommodation.

The Civil Rights Division of the Oregon Bureau of Labor and Industries is responsible for enforcing the state's public accommodation law, and the judge who issued today's proposed order works for the bureau.

In order to reach $135,000, Rachel and Laurel submitted a long list of alleged physical, emotional and mental damages they claim to have experienced as a result of the Kleins' unlawful conduct. One of the women, whose name was redacted to protect her privacy, listed 88 symptoms as grounds for compensation. The other, whose name was also redacted, listed 90.

Examples of symptoms include "acute loss of confidence," "doubt," "excessive sleep," "felt mentally raped, dirty and shameful," "high blood pressure," "impaired digestion," "loss of appetite," "migraine headaches," "pale and sick at home after work," "resumption of smoking habit," "shock" "stunned," "surprise," "uncertainty," "weight gain" and "worry."[13]

The Bowman-Cryers simultaneously lost their appetite and gained weight, in addition to comparing being denied a cake to violent, forcible physical penetration. One of the Kleins' competitors drove down the Kleins' Yelp ratings, flooded social media with nasty comments, and even succeeded in shutting down a GoFundMe fund-raiser for the Kleins, then bragged on Facebook about having done so. I spoke with the Kleins several times, and each time, though through tears, they reiterated that they would fight for their faith. It's important to note that when the incident happened, same-sex marriage was not yet legal in

Oregon; additionally, the Oregon labor commissioner, Brad Avakian (who was behind this judgment against the Kleins) is an outspoken supporter of same-sex marriage and said previously that his goal is to "rehabilitate"[14] businesses that do not accept same-sex marriage.

Barronelle Stutzman is a seventy-year-old grandmother and proprietor of Arlene's Flowers, a business she built with her mother over thirty years ago. I spoke with her on my television program in the spring of 2015. Stutzman was sued into bankruptcy by a longtime client, Robert Ingersoll, whom she had always happily served—until she declined to specifically use her expression for his same-sex wedding ceremony due to her deeply held Christian beliefs. According to her attorney, Kristen Waggoner with Alliance Defending Freedom, "it will take a miracle" for Stutzman to financially survive this. The case is still going through the legal system and Stutzman stands to lose her home. Funds raised for her online are helping.

The fight for equal rights isn't about "equality." It's about attacking faith. Really, this isn't about gay rights. Gay marriage has turned trendy, with the polling changing faster than Caitlyn Jenner at a photo shoot. The Left views the gay community in the same way that it views women: nothing more than a voting bloc. They pay lip service to these demographic groups but never offer anything more beyond decades of inaction. While leftist groups fight for "marriage equality," the Obama administration makes marriage an economic hit with horrible policy. You got bait and switched, leftists! No, the Left has but one goal in mind: Pry the populace from the influence of the church. Every one of these people was attacked more for admitting their Christian beliefs in public than for the threat they posed to anyone's individual rights.

It's hard speaking for truth. Evangelism isn't without struggle. The secular Left has waged every attack upon Christians, and yet so many have stood successfully against it with the backing of the very large and powerful Christian population.

That Christians in this country haven't always known our strengths has been one of our greatest weaknesses.

Last year a friend in Texas whose child attends Keller High School in the Keller Independent School District alerted me to a letter sent out to parents apologizing for an admission made by a motivational speaker named Ryan Roberts. The speaker, a graduate of the school and part of the youth ministry at an area church, spoke to students on dealing with stress and overcoming challenges as part of the C3 Student Leadership Group. He included in his remarks that there was someone in whom they could find peace and relief and asked the students to shout the name of this person on the count of three, yelling "Jesus!" on three. Some found it offensive because there apparently exists the belief that when one person utters the name Jesus in a public setting, a secret magic renders any other diverse thought negligible. People become offended when someone holds a different perspective because in our modern era, not sharing another's point of view is a challenge to that person's character and intelligence. That is how self-serving, insecure, and pathetically whiny people have grown. Roberts apologized on his Facebook page, writing:

> *At the close of the assembly, I spoke on my own accord regarding my personal story and Christian faith with a lack of full awareness of the C3 Student Leadership and*

Keller High School verbal agreement. There was no misunderstanding between the school and the organization as to the topic of the assembly; I accept responsibility for the boundary line that was crossed. This is not an issue of religious liberty; this is a breach of trust between C3 Student Leadership and Keller ISD and for that specifically I sincerely apologize to the students, families, teachers, and administrators affected.[15]

Any "trust" that demands one deny one's Savior isn't a trust.

My staff at the *Blaze* reached out to Roberts to tell this story on my program, but sadly, I was informed by a mutual friend that the church in which he worships did not want what it viewed as bad press, so it instructed him to remain quiet on the issue and allowed the media interest to fade. I was utterly shocked at the decision by a church to pass on an opportunity to witness to the community and also warn its flock about the dangers of secularism to free speech. And yes, I view a publicly funded, government-regulated entity forbidding talk of Jesus as a restriction of speech. When did the church back away from such issues? You will never grow your flock by keeping your witnessing compartmentalized behind the safe-space doors of your building. You will never grow the choir by preaching only to its members. So many churches do such amazing mission work overseas, but too many forget the importance of missionary work in our culture right here at home.

The Bible teaches us to fear many things, but I don't remember bad publicity being one of them.

It has been my personal experience that people of faith often struggle with political witnessing. Because I was raised by Christians as opinionated as me, I've never found it to be a difficulty.

I don't view it as "politicizing" to simply tell the truth. Do we believe that abortion is infanticide? Do we believe that the biblical definition of marriage is a union between one man and one woman? Do we believe that stewardship of our fellow man falls under our domain or under government's domain? Can people of good faith nourish the soul and the body beyond the mediocre allotment of sustenance given by Uncle Sam? My political leanings are not at odds with Jesus's teachings. While it has been Christians who have sheltered the single mother in need, missioned and witnessed to distant lands, given everything they had and more to help their fellow man, it is also the fellowship as a whole that has grown meek, timid, and quiet in the face of a pop-culture assault. Instead of fighting the culture we, with some exceptions, have set ourselves apart from it. Instead of being that light in the darkness we have created our own musical genre, our own production companies, our own films and television channels; we have shrunk from the mainstream pop-cultural sphere, which is insane because *we are cultural.*

I know many Christians who are afraid to engage on this publicly. Every week I have people say to me some variant of "Thank you for doing and saying what you do. I could never do that."

"Why?" is always my response.

"I don't want to lose friends," "I'm not political like that," and "Because it can be divisive" are some of the replies I receive. I'm uninterested in any false unity that dilutes Jesus's sacrifice or God's commandments for us. I'm not here to lie about what God thinks of children in the womb so as to make friends with someone who thinks infanticide is acceptable. I'm uninterested in speaking against godly marriage for the purpose of winning popularity or seeming less "divisive." I'm not divisive. People have *divided themselves* from God. I don't want to widen that gap. I want to close it. I can only do that with truth spoken in love. That's the thing: So many Christians think that politics is a brawl. Yes and no. Responding in a loving manner isn't a reflexive action for me, because I'm imperfect and self-centered. My first (second, and even third) response is all-out war. I don't want to just destroy the argument; I want to destroy the person for making that argument. It's an entirely progressive line of thinking, the last vestige of my liberal upbringing, against which I fight every single day. This is my absolute biggest struggle, my greatest temptation. I struggle most sincerely with separating the person from their argument. I think other Christians fear this too.

Some years ago I had Ephesians 6:12–13 tattooed on my forearm. It was not done to be fashionable. It was a desperate act to remind myself why I do what I do. The verse reads: "For our struggle is not against flesh and blood, but against the rulers, against the authorities, against the powers of this dark world and against the spiritual forces of evil in the heavenly realms. Therefore put on the full armor of God, so that when the day of evil comes, you may be able to stand your ground, and after you have done everything, to stand."

I am not struggling against my fellow man. I am struggling against the evil influences of the world. And when I was once lost, God had mercy on me and grace for me. I cannot expect to win first hearts and then minds in a manner inconsistent with how God Himself pursues us. I also recognize these influences on me and that I'm caving to temptation and ego by submitting to them. If you follow me at all on Twitter, you see that I fail repeatedly. I have come far from where I once was, but the journey is long and I've a promise to keep. I divulge this because I know exactly how politics looks from the outside, especially to the many Christians who don't want that sort of fight. You don't have to have that sort fight. Your fight can look however you want it to look. But as a declared Christian you are in the fight nonetheless. The goal isn't to crush the spirit but to win the heart. The goal isn't to harden hearts with combativeness. A person converted with love in truth is one less person we have to fight.

I know this. I was that person once.

I have to remind myself of this every day, working in the media.

CHAPTER 3

Profiles in Pandering

I hate that what I do is considered part of the media. I hate that I have to share that descriptor with narrative prostitutes who care more about saving the backside of an elected official than about truthfully informing the American public. I was live on air one day for my radio program, and on one of the monitors I saw a bizarre developing story. It was in the aftermath of the San Bernardino terror attack, the one that the media and the Obama administration initially labeled "workplace violence." Reportedly *Inside Edition* had paid the landlord a thousand dollars to pry the plywood from the door of the terrorists' apartment, still apparently an active crime scene, and allow the braying media to stomp and crap all over everything. It was like Black Friday, but with the terrorists' apartment. I watched as one reporter giddily held up to the camera Rafia Farook's driver's license, replete with Social Security number. A member of the San Bernardino Police Department

allegedly responded to questioning about the incident by saying that he was "stunned" the media had just done what it did.
Between prostitution and reporting, nowadays reporting is the
more honorable trade.

Not long before that, during an interview with Anderson
Cooper for his *Anderson Cooper 360°* program, Donald Trump
told Cooper to his face, "The people do not trust you." Trump
added, "I find that 60 percent, 70 percent of the political media
is really, really dishonest." It was rare for any politician to rebuke
a prominent news figure so directly. But on this matter, at least,
Trump was right: As a 2014 Gallup poll showed, Americans'
belief that the media reports the news "fully, accurately, and
fairly" is at an all-time low.[16]

Don't be shocked. This is because much of the news business is really a bunch of multimillionaires faking concern
about Middle America while feeding us narratives that suit
their political agenda. (Spoiler alert: It's almost all elitist and
liberal.) More on that in a moment.

In the town where I grew up, right smack in the middle
of Flyover Nation, you couldn't find a faster, more accurate
source of news than the local grapevine. If I ever got into trouble, I didn't even bother trying to hide it from my mom—
because I knew she would have heard about it long before I got
home. She'd be waiting for me with that look on her face that
told me she already knew the full story, and I might as well
save the explanations. *Everyone* was a narc.

There were two ways the community kept in touch: the Baptist church's lit marquee and the grapevine. They told us who
was getting married, who had died (both), who was pregnant,
who was getting divorced (the grapevine). It's how we learned
about the slap fight in the street in front of the Quik Mart the

same day news broke that one of the churches was building a bigger facility. Information would come our way in bits and pieces over the course of the day—in the bleachers at a high school football game, at the gas station, in the dairy aisle at the grocery store. Keeping one another informed helped us come together to mourn tragedies, like the death of a beloved relative, and celebrate triumphs, like someone's child getting a scholarship to college.

You couldn't just call it gossip, though there might have been some of that involved. It was so much more than that. News traveled fast in my family's small town because we cared about our neighbors. Keeping up with one another fostered the sense of community that we know and love in that part of America that takes up the space between the country's coastlines. More than anything we believed in honesty. When we passed a story up the local grapevine, we did it because it was true and because it brought us closer to the people around us. Also, in my family, because it was highly entertaining to hear my aunts tell it.

Of course, I didn't grow up in the Dark Ages, and despite what some of our coastal cousins certainly think, my America is not a technological desert. Sure, we have TV, radio, the Internet, and even those relics from a bygone era—newspapers. (Isn't it interesting how the snobs at the *New York Times* are clinging to outdated old media with such ferocity? And they call us backward. What Web sites inform *your* view?) But here's the difference: Even when it comes to major national and world events, we pay attention, but we don't live and die by the twenty-four-hour news cycle.

That's because we have lives.

It's hard to be glued to the TV or to Twitter when you're trying to get your kids to soccer practice on time. Pundits on the coasts are constantly filling airtime with their words, and it's hard to pay attention when you're working a double shift at a restaurant, a factory, or a hospital. It's especially hard to perform that Sunday-morning ritual so common in Washington, DC—channel-surfing to catch the highlights from each of the all-important network talk shows—when you're praying for our nation in church. Half of my family never watches when I'm on television, because either (a) they're dirty liberals whom I am required by blood to love or (b) they're working because someone has to pay off entitlements in America.

At best, most of the national media delivering the news to the rest of America experienced our country years ago, so they view us like we view *Star Wars*—something that happened "a long time ago in a galaxy far, far away." That's why I'm often amused—when I'm not ticked off—by multimillionaire anchors and journalists pretending to report on, and care about, the struggles of American families, like the rising prices of gas, groceries, and health insurance. I call them holiday hillbillies. Like those people who go to church only on Christmas, these guys travel out to the heartland only when they need a worn face in a trucker hat to vindicate the opinions they've developed on TV. What's even worse is when they act all high and mighty in reaction to a politician's failure to know the price of a carton of milk or a gallon of gas. True, the politicians are outrageously out of touch, but so are the reporters who are wagging their fingers at them. Just because your second or third home is deep in Flyover and you own two $2,500 Orvis bamboo fly-fishing rods doesn't make you an expert on normal life, Mr. Evening News. And both of these groups—along with all the other classes of consultants, bureaucrats, and strategists—contribute to the constant cycle of noise that powers the twenty-four-hour mainstream-media machine.

The media is supposed to function like our national grapevine. We're supposed to be kept up to speed on the issues of the day, told what's going on around us. But the national media is devoid of much of the honesty, and *all* of the good humor, that drives the human pipelines through which local goings-on travel in the small towns and valleys of Flyover Nation. The major media organizations that provide us with our "news" aren't doing it to help the public become better informed—they're doing it to sell advertising and keep themselves in business. Somebody has to pay for all those anchors' haircuts, after all.

News Anchor Salaries
Chris Cuomo: $2.5 million
Ann Curry: $5 million
Scott Pelley: $5 million
Megyn Kelly: $6 million
Rachel Maddow: $7 million
Shepard Smith: $7–8 million
Brian Williams: $10 million
Anderson Cooper: $11 million
Diane Sawyer: $12 million
Bill O'Reilly: $20 million
Matt Lauer: $25 million[17]

I always wanted to work in media because I liked telling the stories of my community; I was a storyteller. Also, lit majors earn crap, and I wanted to be able to feed myself at some point, so media it was. I always loved to write. It came easily to me, earned scholarships with it and helped pay for college by writing. I enjoyed knitting together sentences, finding the rhythm in a story, really finding the story. Every story can resonate with someone if told simply and honestly. I studied print media in the very early aughts because blogging was still so brand-new. With the help of friends I created a pop-culture Web site titled Anti-Radar, and with a ragtag group of passionate yet unpaid contributors, we covered politics and pop culture with zeal. You could literally watch my growth into a full-fledged conservative on those pages. It was successful enough that I got on promo lists and received tickets to concerts and screenings and access to musicians and actors. One of my favorite interviews was one with the lead singer of VAST in which I learned he had been homeschooled, something I eventually did with my sons. Eventually, as paid freelance writing projects took more and more of my time, I disbanded the Web site. I wrote for various magazines until returning to blogging, this time as a "mom blogger" before the genre became embarrassingly, grotesquely overcommercialized and trite. I called (and trademarked) the site *Mamalogues*, and on it I came to terms with being a young mother in the city. I was eventually offered a weekly column in the daily paper and did radio hits with various stations across the country. I taped an episode for a travel show on the Style channel and appeared on Wendy Williams's NYC-based television program several times. During my transformation from a liberal into a conservative, I didn't write much about politics.

Slowly, as I became more involved, I began a second blog, anonymously, titled *Keyboard Pundit*. I wrote for myself and opined on political issues of the day. I knew that my *Mamalogues* audience—which included both conservatives and progressives

of St. Louis, Francis Slay)—would not respond
onal political revolution. It was a good gig. I
s for the site, I was called a "new Erma Bombeck,"
won awards, including a best of from the alternative weekly. It was harder to hide what was taking place
personally, however. I was, and am to this day, honest and accessible in my writing. It was becoming more difficult to hide my
political conversion, especially as we were in the waning years of
the Bush era. I began crashing progressive protests. I went alone
to one protest where progressives had assembled outside across
from the convention center where the American Legion was having its annual event. I watched as elderly vets exited the building
and saw protesters yelling at them, holding vile anti-Bush plac-
ards, and burning American flags. It made me think of my grandfather, a navy vet. My cousin, an army vet who served in Iraq. One
protester tried to set fire to an American flag next to me; I grabbed
it and stomped out the flame. Cops intervened. One handed me a
bottle of water. I thanked him for his service. And that was it.

One of my columns in the daily paper addressed guns in the
home. I wrote a focused piece on firearm ownership and how it
was something in which we believed, hardly controversial. It
was the first and last time that I underestimated the antigun
outrage brigade. They lost their ever-loving minds and demanded
that the paper drop me. I was told by my editor that I was "too
forward," but really the objection was that my column articu-
lated a conservative viewpoint that was foreign to the newspaper and its heavily progressive blue-haired subscribers. We
parted ways and for a time it was a local-media bonanza, with
the alternative weekly, the daily's archenemy, gleefully mocking
the newspaper for its actions. Later the alternative weekly put
me on its cover for a fair and well-written story authored by

Kristen Hinman. At this time, shortly before the 2008 elections, I had been offered a radio program with the powerhouse talk station in St. Louis. On air I cofounded the Tea Party movement in my town. During this time my disdain for media grew.

The Tea Party's treatment at the hands of the so-called fair and impartial media was abhorrent. For a long time they ignored us. Then they mocked us. Then they called us fascists and racists and homophobes. They called us angry and stupid. Then they wrote our obituary the minute any Tea Party candidate lost any election anywhere. They made up stories (remember the fabricated John Lewis slur?). MSNBC once cropped out a gun-toting tea partier at a rally because said gun-toting tea partier was black. They said that the Tea Party was nothing but a weak flash in the pan while simultaneously blaming our massive influence for wrecking their agenda. They couldn't pick a narrative. They were just as petty covering Republican candidates during the election. Once, in a sign of its total arrogance, the liberal *Huffington Post* huffily announced that Donald Trump—who at the time had the support of as many as 30 percent of Republicans—would be covered only on the entertainment pages. Think what you will of Trump, but it's not up to the *Huffington Post*, which hasn't the first clue about the conservative movement, to dictate to Republicans which candidates they should and should not take seriously. It would be like the *New York Times* deciding that Hillary Clinton should be discussed only in the metro crime section of the paper. (Actually, that's not a bad idea.)

Not all networks are as contemptuous of Americans, of course. For instance, at the *Blaze*, where I work, we do things a little bit differently. Glenn Beck calls it "The Network YOU Are Building" for a reason. Our individual subscribers are not only the backbone of our support; they are our very reason for existence. Maybe you're one of them. Maybe you're one of the hundreds of thousands of supporters who make getting up and doing what I do every day worthwhile. And wouldn't you know it—most of our subscribers live in Flyover Nation.

But let's talk about the other folks. Let's talk about the folks in the mainstream media who are supposed to be the opinion makers and influencers that the rest of us slack-jawed yokels must listen to with rapt attention as they tell us what to think. At least, that's what *they* think of us. That's because "they"—reporters, commentators, and other "media personalities," especially at the big cable news stations—live in a different world from the rest of us. Some of them were virtually born into this rarefied sphere, and others found their way from humbler beginnings. But they're all firmly on the same team now—and it's not yours and mine.

These titans of media have very little use for the average American, except as a support system for a pair of eyeballs that can watch TV, thereby leading to higher ratings and purchases of advertisers' products (not to mention feeding the ego engines that drive these so-called journalists). They prefer to live and work only in one another's company. They cluster together in enclaves in New York City, where the media is a $19.7 billion business and set to jump to $23.6 billion by 2018.[18] They even vacation together in tony resort communities like Martha's Vineyard, where the average house on the market fetches more than $2.1 million.[19]

If your job is to report the news for all Americans, how can you understand your audience if your entire existence is confined to this rarefied world? If the realities of daily life in most of this country—whether to buy hot dogs or frozen pizza at the grocery store, or how much longer your tank of gas will *really* last when it says it's on empty—are so foreign to you after decades of life at the top, should you really be the one to interpret world events for the rest of us? And more important, why should anyone listen to you?

The elite journalists love to grill other people, like members of Congress and political candidates, about how well they understand Americans. If I were running a major media company, I'd ask anyone who wanted to be on TV or have a byline in a publication the same questions. Here are just a few I think Flyover Americans would love to hear Chris Cuomo or Katie Couric's answers to:

Questions for the Media Elite

1. When was the last time you dined by choice at Country Buffet? Or IHOP?
2. Name a country music song.
3. When did you last drive an American-made car?
4. How do you clean a whitetail?
5. How much does an average American pay for a mortgage? And how much do you pay? (Please include all homes.)
6. When did you have to buy your own health insurance?
7. What goes on a Big Mac?
8. Do you take vacations in any of the following: Martha's Vineyard, the Hamptons, Nantucket?
9. Do your children attend public school?
10. Name six products you can buy at Walmart and estimate the prices.
11. Who is Hank Hill?
12. Identify Indiana on a map.

13. *Name a current NASCAR driver.*
14. *Have you ever entered a Men's Wearhouse or Dress Barn (other than for a feature story)?*
15. *What is your pastor's name?*
16. *Name a Republican presidential candidate for whom you ever voted.*
17. *How do you take your grits?*
18. *Bonus: What is a grit?*
19. *Have you ever worn bags over socks in regular shoes because you didn't have snow boots?*
20. *Why are you such a douche bag?*

It's not just that the media elites are out of touch. They are also contemptuous of the very Americans they pretend to report the news to, be accountable to, and champion. Some examples:

Exhibit 1: NBC, the Network for Nitwits, Brats, and Clueless Trust-Fund Babies

Say you need a job and, like most millennials, aren't qualified to do anything. You could look for a low-paying entry-level job. However, if you're an overeducated rich kid with no real-world experience who's lived off your family's name and money all your life, the answer is easy: Go to work for NBC "News." It pays the entitled and well connected a small fortune every year to put on makeup and pretend to be hard-hitting journalists.

How pathetic it must be to be a reporter or producer at NBC News these days. You studied journalism in college, worked a string of crappy jobs just to make it to New York or DC, get paid a terrible salary to be in the presence of journalistic titans—and then you have to sit there while Luke Russert or Chelsea Clinton wanders in, sits in front of a camera, and earns ten times your salary because of who their daddy was.

There's a lot of nepotism in journalism and NBC is not the only offender. So maybe it's a little unfair to single out Chelsea Clinton for criticism. But let's do it anyway. She deserves it.

Here's the thing about Chelsea Clinton, the daughter of two of the biggest money-grubbing con artists in American history. She was a total disaster as an NBC employee—and everyone knows it. The former first daughter—dubbed "the royal child" by those with the misfortune of "working" with her—earned hundreds of thousands of dollars a year to do basically nothing. Don't take my word for it. In 2014 *New York* magazine called Chelsea's NBC deal "an unbelievably cushy fake job" and reported she'd earned $600,000 per year, or $27,272 for every minute she was on the air (a total of twenty-two minutes all year long).

"Chelsea's storytelling inspired people across the country and showcased the real power we have as individuals to make a difference in our communities," said NBC News senior vice president Alex Wallace, who, if there's any justice in this world, is out of a job by now.[20]

Maybe NBC hired Chelsea for all of her real-world experience, said no one. Like her days hanging around Oxford. Or her make-work job at her daddy's foundation, where she can pretend to save the world while making everyone else's life there a living hell.[21]

Chelsea once told a British newspaper she didn't care about money.[22] She has the luxury of saying that, since her parents paid for her $3 million wedding and $10 million apartment in New York City. And NBC paid her to—well, whatever it is that she actually did all day. Unfortunately, Chelsea departed NBC in the fall of 2014 so she could run her mother's campaign for president into the ground. Keep up the good work, Chelsea!

NBC should be ashamed of itself. But it isn't. It does this all the time. NBC hired Jenna Bush for such hard-hitting segments as interviewing her grandmother, Barbara, on her ninetieth birthday. And it brought on Luke Russert, twenty-three years old at the time, because it felt bad for him after his dad, actual journalist Tim Russert, died.

"I know what kids are going through, and I try to bring that perspective," said Russert, the millionaire heir of two wealthy journalists, who attended the elite St. Albans School in Washington, DC (tuition: $33,000 per year). Yes, Russert knows about the hard choices America's young people face these days—like whether to take tennis or yachting lessons and how to properly address one of your fellow classmates, Sabah al-Sabah, a member of the Kuwaiti royal family.

And it won't be long before Malia or Sasha Obama shows up to provide "exclusive" interviews with her dad once he's out of the White House. I can't wait.

Exhibit 2: Diane Sawyer, Liberalism's Go-To Girl

While she no longer has a show of her own, Diane Sawyer remains one of the most recognizable faces on television. The former anchor of the *ABC World News* evening broadcast is still regularly called upon to conduct big-name interviews, such as her blockbuster April 2015 sit-down with the Celebrity Formerly Known as Bruce Jenner. I once joined her for the night to cover the 2010 midterm elections. With her serious but personable demeanor, Sawyer has been a presence on network news for decades. It seems to have worked out for her: Sawyer reportedly now has a net worth of approximately $80 million.[23]

That amount of money is almost inconceivable to most Americans, but believe it or not, Diane Sawyer's origins lie squarely within the borders of Flyover Nation. She was born in Glasgow, Kentucky, and raised in Louisville; her mother was a teacher, and her father was a World War II veteran who was active in local politics—as a Republican.

The ambitious seventeen-year-old made her way to Wellesley College in Massachusetts. Wellesley may be better known today as an incubator of surly, shower-averse radical feminists—and, of course, Hillary Clinton—but it has long enjoyed a reputation for educating the daughters of the East Coast elite. Diane Sawyer felt a little out of place in these august surroundings. She felt different from her more sophisticated classmates, but she was determined to remain true to her roots. "When the other girls were getting packages of Krön chocolates," she recounted in a 1984 interview, "I was sent turnips and tomatoes from home—beautifully wrapped."[24]

After graduation in 1967, she went home to try her hand at journalism. Her first job was as the weather girl at a local Louisville TV station. She eventually became a reporter but didn't stick around for long. In 1970 she went east to Washington, DC, to work as a press aide in Richard Nixon's White House. Perhaps not surprising for the daughter of a local Republican politician, but still eyebrow raising given the slant of Sawyer's later reporting, this move was her first foray into the world of the coastal elites. After all, working in the White House can lead to many lucrative career options later on. Washington is full of "former administration officials" who trade on their former titles and contact lists and never seem to run out of cocktail parties.

If Nixon's had been a typical administration, the future might have turned out quite differently for the young press aide from Louisville whom the president called the "smart girl."[25] Of course, the Nixon White House was anything but typical. Nixon resigned on August 9, 1974, and retreated to California. Among the former White House staff who followed him to the other coast was Diane Sawyer, who spent the next four years helping the disgraced former president write his memoirs. Why did she stick by him? Sawyer later said: "I stayed from a sense of duty and obligation and concern for a human being who was in a crisis."[26]

In 1978 she left Nixonland and returned to TV journalism, taking a job as a reporter for CBS News. This was where her ascent really began. She rose rapidly at CBS and in 1984 became the first female reporter ever to join the venerable *60 Minutes* program. She moved to ABC in 1989 and spent twenty years hosting such shows as *20/20* and *Good Morning America* before taking over the *World News* anchor desk in 2009. She stepped down from that position in 2014.

Especially since her move to ABC, the former Republican White House staffer—who stayed with her Republican boss even after he resigned from office—appears to have given more of her favor to Democrats. As the Media Research Center notes:

> *At ABC, Sawyer has repeatedly lauded high-profile liberals, including Nancy Pelosi ("galvanized steel with a smile") and Hillary Clinton ("political mastery," "dazzling"). She even admitted to co-host Charlie Gibson that she dreamed about Bill Clinton one night after then*

eating a pepperoni pizza . . . She derided the Bush admin-
istration's "massive tax cuts," championed campaign
finance "reform," and even asked then-candidate Barack
Obama to judge whether America is "more racist or more
sexist."[27]

She also referred to a speech by Senator Ted Kennedy at the
2008 Democratic National Convention as "an incredible night . . .
a return and a roar from the lion of the Democrats."[28]

Whatever her own political preferences, Sawyer portrayed
herself as a reporter who cared, one who was fearlessly rooting
for you, the underdog of the Flyover Nation. This was on view,
for instance, in her *Hidden America* special, which sought to
spotlight, among other groups of noncoastal Americans,
female prison inmates and poor children in Appalachia. Sawyer claimed that she "and her crew" traveled fourteen thousand miles over two years to do the report. Care to guess how
many of those miles were actually experienced by Sawyer and
how many by "her crew"? All in all, Sawyer's foray into Appalachia was a farce. It was impossible for her to conceal her
bewilderment and contempt for the state she once called home.
She portrayed the citizens of eastern Kentucky as if they were
joyless, drug-addled fools and toothless moms who used trash
cans as toilets, never washed their children, and danced for
rain. She pranced around towns as if she expected zombies to
jump out of the windows. The mayor of the town of Hazard
called the documentary "the same load of crap they've been
doing for 40 years."[29]

Maybe the fact that Sawyer and her team referred to the citizens of Appalachia as "hidden" suggests the distance that had
developed between her and the people she intended to cover.

Poverty and prison can be unfortunate facts of life and wreak havoc on communities all across America. Diane Sawyer might briefly explore that world, but her own was very different.

When Sawyer left ABC *World News* in August 2014, she was reportedly earning $20 million per year.[30] In 1988 she had married successful movie director Mike Nichols, whose total net worth was estimated at about $20 million upon his death.[31] Sawyer and Nichols had what can only be described as a fairy-tale romance for the coastal elite—they met in Paris as they were preparing to board the Concorde, the supersonic jet that ferried high rollers across the Atlantic Ocean in about three hours.[32] Sawyer and Nichols were married in her native Kentucky—just kidding! Actually the festivities took place on Martha's Vineyard, a favorite retreat of the eastern establishment and entertainment. The Obamas and Clintons are frequent Vineyard visitors, as are singers James Taylor and Carly Simon and former late-night host David Letterman.[33] Sawyer's onetime *60 Minutes* colleague Mike Wallace put his Vineyard house on the market for $7.8 million in 2011—for that price he offered a six-bedroom home on 1.4 acres, including a private beach.[34] The bicoastal couple also maintained a home in Santa Barbara, along with residences in Connecticut and Manhattan—where, according to a *People* magazine profile, they were known as "one of New York's reigning power couples."[35] But the exclusive Martha's Vineyard appears to have held special significance for them. When Nichols died in 2014, the local paper recounted their ties to the place:

> *Mr. Nichols, with his wife, Diane Sawyer, former anchor of ABC News, were longtime seasonal residents of Martha's Vineyard. The couple were married on the Island*

in 1988, and in 1995 purchased Chip Chop, the former home of actress Katharine Cornell, located overlooking Vineyard Sound on the west side of the entrance to Lake Tashmoo.[36]

Chip Chop and Lake Tashmoo are a world away from Louisville, Kentucky. But on the Vineyard maybe the Kentucky girl who got vegetables delivered to Wellesley while her classmates got gourmet chocolates finally feels like she belongs. After all, you can't get much farther from Flyover Nation.

Exhibit 3: George Stephanopoulos, the Clintons' Media Apologist

Did you hear that George Stephanopoulos just signed a new deal with ABC? He'll remain the host of *Good Morning America* until 2021, for the princely fee of $105 million. His cohost on the set, Robin Roberts, makes $14 million a year, just so they can read words that other far less well-paid people have written down for them about things most of us don't really care about.

Just the other week, for example, the program offered not one, not two, but three different segments on Kermit the Frog's breakup with Miss Piggy. This, of course, provided millions in free advertising for the upcoming Muppets TV series debuting on . . . surprise, surprise . . . ABC. Promoting *The Muppets* not only helps ABC's ratings but also gives big bucks to the Walt Disney Company, which owns *The Muppets*, the ABC network, and thus *Good Morning America*. Frankly, if some company wants to pay two Democrats millions of dollars to pretend to report the news without bias or to care about the average American while flacking for the corporation that owns them, well, that's capitalism for you. But I don't think the rest of us should be fooled. These people know little about the concerns of average Americans and, what's more, look down on most of us anyway from the safety of their high-rise apartments in Manhattan or their summer homes in the Hamptons.

Stephanopoulos served as a loyal Democrat operative for many years on Capitol Hill, in the campaign world, and eventually in the Clinton White House. It was his work on the 1992 Clinton campaign and in the White House that made Stephanopoulos's name, and it appears he has been only too eager to look out for his friends the Clintons in return.

But before all of that, Stephanopoulos was a kid growing up in a Greek American family in the suburbs of Cleveland. His father was a Greek Orthodox priest, and both of his parents were themselves first-generation American citizens.[37] Young George had ambitions beyond the suburbs. He went to New York City for college and studied political science at Columbia, after which he received a Rhodes Scholarship to Oxford University. When he got back from England, Stephanopoulos headed where lots of undergraduate political science majors go to make names for themselves—Washington, DC, specifically Capitol Hill. Stephanopoulos joined the staff of Cleveland-area Democratic congressman Ed Feighan. He eventually became chief of staff, Feighan's top aide, in charge of the rest of the office.

By 1988 his ambition had grown beyond the Hill. He left Feighan's office to work on Michael Dukakis's presidential campaign. Like Stephanopoulos, Dukakis was both a Greek American and a committed liberal. Dukakis lost the 1988 election to then–vice president George H. W. Bush, but the experience gave Stephanopoulos a taste for campaign work.

He returned to Capitol Hill in 1989 and served as a floor assistant in the office of House majority leader Dick Gephardt. Floor assistants are a rare breed—a small handful of staffers with House leadership offices are permitted on the floor of the House chamber along with members in order to help the processes run smoothly. Considering the state of Washington, DC, over the last several years, maybe the floor assistants should be doing some things differently.

Perhaps the life of a floor assistant was not all that glamorous—George Stephanopoulos did not remain one for very long. In 1991 he jumped to another campaign, this one for the governor of Arkansas, Bill Clinton. Stephanopoulos headed up the campaign's communications efforts, and this time his team won. And the victor got the spoils: After Clinton's 1992 win, George Stephanopoulos walked into the White House as senior adviser to the president on policy and strategy and continued to deal with the press extensively. While he was in the White House, a film was released that helped solidify an image of Stephanopoulos as one of the bright young political minds that were taking over Washington along with their charismatic new president. *The War Room*, a documentary filmed at Clinton headquarters and at various campaign stops, was released in 1993, and the elites fawned over the two staffers who received the most screen time—Stephanopoulos and strategist James Carville. The *New York Times* called Stephanopoulos "the brilliant, handsome Rhodes Scholar who . . . calmly but surely mobilizes his staff to take the presidency."[38] The film was hailed as "a compelling and enlightening adventure story about two remarkable men [Stephanopoulos and Carville], and about the monumental effort, determination and chutzpah that is required to conduct and win a political campaign in the modern age."[39]

But even the George Stephanopouloses of the world run out of "determination and chutzpah" at times. In 1996, just after President Clinton was reelected to another term, Stephanopoulos left the White House. A 1999 report following the publication of Stephanopoulos's book *All Too Human* described the cause of his departure as "'burnout' so draining he sought psychiatric help." A therapist prescribed him antidepressant medication in 1995, but he was able to stop taking the drugs upon leaving DC for a "less pressured" life in New York.[40]

It was here that Stephanopoulos started working as a political analyst for ABC News in 1997. He provided commentary on its *This Week* program, and in 2002 he took over as host of the show himself. With a brief interruption between 2010 and 2012, Stephanopoulos has been at *This Week* ever since. He also cohosts *Good Morning America* and holds the title of "Chief Anchor" at ABC.[41] By 2014, Stephanopoulos had amassed a net worth of $18 million.[42] But money, it seems, can't buy journalistic integrity.

In the spring of 2015, controversy raged around the shady donors and fund-raising practices of the Clinton Foundation, as Hillary Clinton, seeking the Democratic nomination for president in 2016, tried to defend her group's acceptance of foreign donations while she was the sitting secretary of state. There's nothing new about politicians taking money from anyone and everyone, but seeing as how the nation's top diplomat was involved with another group that took millions from foreign governments, this was big news. George Stephanopou-los put on his journalist hat and earnestly reported on the alle-gations.

As it turned out, he wasn't exactly giving the full story to the American people—or even to his own network. Stepha-nopoulos neglected to share that he himself was in fact a sub-stantial donor to the Clinton Foundation, having forked over $75,000 between 2012 and 2014.[43] He did not disclose this to ABC, nor did he think it necessary to mention it directly to his viewers as he reported on the foundation's difficulties. There was certainly no mention of Stephanopoulos's own donation history when he sat down for an interview with Peter Schwei-zer, author of the book *Clinton Cash: The Untold Story of How and Why Foreign Governments and Businesses Helped Make Bill and Hillary Rich*, in April 2015. Stephanopoulos got feisty in defense of his old friends the Clintons, telling Schwei-zer, "We've done investigative work here at ABC News [and] found no proof of any kind of direct action" by the then secre-tary of state. "I still haven't heard any direct evidence," the former Clinton spokesman continued, "and you just said you had no evidence that she intervened here."[44]

Just two days after his combative interview with Schweizer, Stephanopoulos discussed the controversy in friendly territory in an appearance on *The Daily Show*, the liberal Mt. Sinai from which the elites' preferred prophet, Jon Stewart, dished out his sanctimonious—allegedly funny—commentary until recently. A triumphant Stephanopoulos told Stewart:

> *I read the book that this is based on,* Clinton Cash, *and I actually interviewed the author on Sunday. This is a*

*tough one. Because when you actually look at, look
closely at it, he even says there is no evidence of any
direct action taken on behalf of the donors.*[45]

He did allow for the possibility that maybe the donors had
some benefits in mind: "Everybody also knows when those
donors give that money, President Clinton or someone, they
get a picture with him, there is a hope that is going to lead to
something."[46] But at no point did he mention his own donations to the foundation (or whether he got a picture with his
former boss in return).

Just weeks later, in mid-May, the news of Stephanopoulos's
own donations broke. He defended himself with spin worthy
of his days on the campaign trail or at the White House. He
said he made the donations "for the best reasons" and hadn't
thought it necessary to tell anyone because he "believed that
the donations already were a matter of public record." In true
Beltway insider fashion, he admitted wrongdoing while still
maintaining he had done nothing wrong:

> *At the time I did not perceive the problem, but in retro-
> spect, as much as I support the very good work that's
> been done by the foundation, I should have gone above
> and beyond any guidelines to make sure that there
> wouldn't be any appearance of any conflict.*[47]

He ended up making public apologies on both of his shows,
Good Morning America and *This Week*.

It's hard to figure out which is the most perverse aspect of
the whole Stephanopoulos saga. Was it venerating a shameless
political hack into a national celebrity? Was it placing him in a

position of authority to read the news to the rest of us rubes? Considering all of this, is anyone surprised that he's still funneling money to his former bosses? In politics, especially in the orbit of cult figures like the Clintons, sycophantic loyalty is valued above all else.

It's important to remember that not only is our country run by a lot of people who never visit Middle America, but many of them actually grew up in Flyover and couldn't wait to get away from it. Thankfully, in Flyover Nation we can tell right from wrong. Maybe it's because we work for our living, unlike Stephanopoulos, who is still trading on his past as a political operative. We know that we can't show up for work every day and do our job with anything other than absolute honesty. And George Stephanopoulos betrayed the trust the public placed in him as a journalist when he went to bat for the Clintons, just as he made his name doing years ago. Most of us in Flyover Nation can recognize when a leopard's spots haven't changed.

I don't deserve credit for saying Oprah Winfrey thinks she's Jesus. That honor goes to comedian and notorious but-her-face Kathy Griffin, who poked fun at the former talk show host's self-appointment as America's self-help guru. There's plenty of evidence that Kathy Griffin is right. Admirers have discussed whether Oprah is a messiah.[48] Oprah's mission statement, she pompously announced, is "to be a teacher."[49] Oprah even nicknamed her $52 million estate in California—complete with its own contemplative teahouse—"the Promised Land."[50] Now that I think about it, Oprah really is a lot like Jesus. That is, if Christ had built a following among people searching for a better life and then financed a billion-dollar empire off their misery and loneliness while politically supporting things Scripture opposed.

In truth, the religion she's starting is very close to what Christianity would look like if you removed every reference to the Father, the Son, or the Holy Spirit.

Here's the thing about Oprah. She is a true Flyover native; she was born poor in Mississippi and experienced a rough upbringing. She was raised by a single mom, was raped at age nine, and gave birth to a baby when she was fourteen years old. (Sadly, the baby later died.)

It makes perfect sense that Oprah would want to leave all that far, far behind. Who wouldn't want to wipe the slate? The problem is she keeps coming back and making everyone else's life a mess. Beneath her optimism-filled self-help mumbo jumbo lurks a real contempt for Flyover country. We're the ones who make her famous and rich—and she can't get enough of it. For what other reason does one of the world's richest women—a billionaire three times over—charge regular Joes anywhere from $99 to $999 just to get a ticket to one of her silly self-help tours that massage her ego? Why else does she encourage people to waste their hard-earned money on her latest "favorite thing," such as headphones that cost $700 (pennies to her), foot cream, a giant box of flowers for $189, or a custom dog bed with your animal's face printed on it?[51] Does she actually think anyone in the real world needs to spend $250 for a box to hold their glasses? How many glasses does she think a person owns? She once even listed one of her own books as a favorite thing—so more people would buy it.[52]

Why else would she fill people's heads with a bunch of kooky, new age blatherings that she thinks are profound? "I know now that I must validate myself before I want others to validate me."

"I know that it's okay to have my own opinions and tell the truth." "I know I am a product of what I believe to be true." These are the kinds of things homeless people mutter on street corners—we don't pay them a hundred bucks to hear it. Oprah's "The Life You Want" tour is from start to finish a cruel hoax. Its very name suggests that listening to Oprah can bring you her success. Let me save you some money. Here's how you can be like Oprah: Build a time machine, become a fat black woman on Chicago television doing shows about Siamese twins and people finding out their sister is their mother, and then wait. Listening to her tell others how to be successful is like listening to a lottery winner tell people how they made a fortune. *She had some talent and she got lucky.* End of lesson.

Maybe because she's feeling guilty that she's made it so big, Oprah is in constant search of a reason for her luxurious life. Surely it's happened so that she can save the world?

She hasn't.

For one thing, she inflicted Dr. Phil on the rest of America—a modern-day huckster who has been sued multiple times for bizarre behavior and reckless endangerment of his foolish flock of Flyover followers.[53] His insurance company agreed to pay $10 million after a group of devotees said he misled them about his diet shakes and bars—called "Shape Up!"—another Oprah-style effort to fleece regular people under the guise of improving their lives.[54]

Prominent physicians demanded the dismissal of another of Oprah's discoveries, Mehmet Oz, for misleading and endangering the public with what they said were false statements about genetically modified foods.[55] Oprah herself started a "leadership academy" in South Africa, to much media praise, even though the $40 million she supposedly spent on things like high-thread-count sheets, theaters, and a beauty parlor so she could show off to her friends might actually have been used to, oh, I don't know, save entire villages? The worst part about it is that Oprah, in the slimy tradition of snake oil salesmen and televangelists everywhere, is still ripping her followers off to this very day. Why does a billionaire need an online merch division? A magazine with her name on it? An entire cable channel? Don't misunderstand me, I love capitalism as much as the next person, but *dang.* There is a line between capitalism and worship. She sells DVDs of her films online. She sells mugs with the obnoxious, Jesus-like phrase "Peace. Love. Oprah"—for $22. And for $38 you can buy a cheesy shirt with the same slogan, "oversized." Ahem. She charges money for "courses" with famous friends like ultrarich Arianna Huffington, who for $49.99 does a pretaped lecture on how regular Americans can "thrive." *Thrive* also happens to be the name of Huffington's book, which you can also purchase. Arianna doesn't have time for an entire "course" with you Flyover fools, so she contracts out her advice with videotaped segments from other rich people like Kobe Bryant and "happiness expert" Shawn Achor, who offers his own class for $99.

Still think Oprah cares about you? Well, she is leaving her dogs—her dogs— $30 million in her will. I have dogs. I love my dogs. I would not leave my dogs $30 million because they are *dogs.*

Oprah thinks we're idiots. And judging by all the people still flocking to Her Greatness for a morsel of nonsense pie, she's right.

CHAPTER 4

Defending American Exceptionalism

All this—for a flag?
—Michelle Obama

Fourth of July, Flyover Country, USA. There's no other party quite like it anywhere in the world.

Patriotism is celebrated with classic middle-American pageantry. That's because in that part of the country, it's still a valued virtue of everyday life—and an opportunity to do some good for the community. There's nothing quite like celebrating the spirit of America's founding to bring folks together to take care of their own.

It's hard to say what hits you first. Maybe it's the heat—the muggy thickness of it in Georgia or the dry, crisp air of Texas.

Maybe it's the smells—asphalt mingling with fresh-cut grass, all covered by the sweet and spicy smoke rising from grills of all shapes and sizes. Maybe it's the colors, only three—red, white, and blue, and plenty of each. Or maybe it's the sounds— engines humming, children screaming excitedly, a few scales or strains of "The Stars and Stripes Forever" as the high school band warms up. As you take it all in, it's clear you're celebrating America's birthday in Flyover Nation. And as far as I'm concerned, on that special day there's no better place to be.

In my family's hometown nestled in the Ozarks, there exists one big holiday: Freedom Fest. The people in town are so proud of it they made themselves a giant wooden sign that says HOME OF THE FREEDOM FEST, and people driving through think, *What?*

Freedom Fest is the town's happy-birthday-America party. There are flags all over the place—on street signs, lampposts, telephone poles—there can never be too many. Red-white-and-blue bunting hangs from the windows of buildings all up and down the street, along with banners with simple, heartfelt messages: GOD BLESS AMERICA or THANK YOU, VETERANS. There's that light breeze that makes the flags and banners wave slightly as it brings some relief from the heat.

The breeze also carries the smells—gas from the cars and trucks and fire engines idling as they wait for the parade to start, concrete and blacktop being baked by the sun, and the food. When I was a kid my entire family was in the parade; in fact, I remember practically the entire town being in the parade so there weren't really that many people left to watch it. Everyone dressed up as either Uncle Sam, Lady Liberty, or a clown, because clowns are easy. My cousin told me all he had to do was get into our aunt's makeup kit and smear her blue eye shadow over half his face and—ta-da!—instant clown. In the parking lots off Main Street, in front of the bank, the post office, and the Rest'urnt, the master chefs are at work. Truck beds are down and grills are blazing. Hot dogs, hamburgers, and chicken are all cooked up and served up any way you like. Every grill master has their own special marinade or trick to knowing just the right time to flip the meat, often passed down from parents or grandparents. They will fight you to protect the recipe. My grandma used to make her famous chicken and dumplings from scratch, and she always lied to people who asked her for the recipe because she was so competitive. She took it to her grave. There's corn on the cob, rubbed with plenty of butter and salt and pepper. There are piles of potato salad and steaming vats of baked beans. There are fresh vegetables from your neighbors' backyards—the basics like lettuce, tomato, and onion. You'd have a tough time finding kale or arugula at this kind of cookout. No one talks about gluten. During a recent visit I mentioned that I ate paleo and didn't eat gluten due to my husband's sensitivity, and a cousin asked if gluten sensitivity was like AIDS.

Paper plates are passed among the throngs of people gathered in the parking lots and lined up along the street. All of the shops are closed. Store stoops, curbs, and sidewalks have turned into bleachers for the show to come. There's anticipation, but there's no sense of rush. Folks in Flyover Nation don't do a whole lot of rushing around—they prefer to leave the business of running around like headless chickens to their cousins on the coasts. The time is "whenever you get there." Especially today. Right now they're content to catch up with their friends and neighbors, their kids' teachers, church friends they haven't had the chance to talk to in a couple of hours. It seems like everyone in town has turned out for the celebration—and that's because they have.

The Fourth of July is truly a community event in Flyover Nation. Not only does everyone come out to be part of the festivities, but everyone has pitched in to help get them up and running. The First Baptist Church's quilting circle made the patriotic bunting that hangs from every windowsill and porch. The Methodists have a stand set up in their parking lot serving lemonade and iced tea. Mrs. Jones's third-grade class made the red-white-and-blue paper fans hanging from the truck beds. The owner of the Quik-Mart is in charge of the turtle races. The high school cheerleaders got together to paint the mural that depicts the founding of our country and thanks those who've served in the military for their sacrifices. Maybe their renditions of Washington and Jefferson and Franklin aren't the most true to life, but there's no doubting the amount of heart they put into the project. That's the theme for the decorations that have gone up all across town. They're simple, honest, and homemade. They stick to the basics—red, white, and blue. We don't need any more glitz and glamour than that. Nobody is trying to outdo one another with flash and glitter, though there's always a hint of friendly competition with the parade in the next town over. Anyway, most of the "flash" is being saved for the fireworks display later in the evening.

A few triumphant notes from the high school band tell the assembled crowds the parade is under way. The band leads the procession, complete with baton twirlers and the school's ROTC color guard bearing Old Glory out in front. Then come the mayor and the city council members, putting aside their politicking for once to enjoy the day. A fire truck follows, lights flashing silently—this time for entertainment, not an emergency.

There are plenty of other groups—Boy Scouts, Girl Scouts, the guys who restore vintage cars and live for the days when they can show off their Mustangs or Corvettes or ancient Studebakers at events like this. Some towns are lucky enough to have few Shriners zip past in their miniature cars, tossing candy to kids. But the most powerful moment of the entire proceeding comes when the veterans pass by. These are the men—and women too— who left the ranks of the community to go answer their country's call and were lucky enough to return. The oldest among them defeated fascism, joining up after Pearl Harbor and going on to break the Nazi stranglehold on Europe or island-hop across the Pacific toward Japan. Others fought communism on the battlefields of Korea and Vietnam—to them, the "cold war" was plenty hot. The youngest among them might have just returned from fighting terrorism in Afghanistan or Iraq. Now they wear their American Legion or Veterans of Foreign Wars caps and march proudly past. Some of the very old are in wheelchairs, pushed along by their younger comrades.

It is for these heroes of the past and present that the loudest cheers go up. Flyover Nation sends many of its citizens to fight for the United States. In these towns in Middle America, military service is a serious obligation and a point of pride. It's family history. This pride is personal. Everyone in the community wants to make sure these veterans know just how much their sacrifice is appreciated. These "boys," as they're always called, no matter what their age, are our own. We're the friends and neighbors of these veterans. Some of us taught them in grade school or sat next to them in church. As we cheer for those who came back and are marching in today's parade, we make sure to cheer extra loudly so the ones who didn't make it home can hear us too.

After the parade finishes, the cookouts simmer down, and the sun begins to set, everyone gradually moves toward the park near the center of town or, in my family's town's case, the parking lot of the Rest'urnt. A flatbed was brought in earlier and the country band is setting up to play. In other small Flyover towns, families have brought blankets to lie on the grass. Dogs and children, of course, have no interest in lying down anywhere and proceed to chase each other gleefully. Maybe the band, now seated, is still playing, or maybe someone is singing patriotic songs. Some of the local thespians from the community theater group might give an impassioned reading of the Declaration of Independence.

Once it's dark, the fireworks show begins. The charges explode with brilliant blasts, sending shimmering showers of red, white, blue, green, orange, and yellow falling down the night sky. Everyone, from the youngest to the oldest resident, stares up in awe. From somewhere, whether played live or piped in on speakers, the "1812 Overture" plays for the finale. A deep and powerful sense of pride is felt by everyone watching this scene play out in countless towns across America, especially in Flyover country.

In my family's hometown the local fire station came up with a clever way to raise money on the Fourth of July that ended up being fun for the whole family. After the parade, while everyone was still milling around downtown, you could head over to the small firehouse, put a dollar in the bucket, and engage in some good old-fashioned, wholesome destruction. They'd give you a bat, and you could take a few swings at an old car. By the end of the day, that junker was bashed up beyond all recognition. Kids just loved smashing things, grown men loved to show off their strength, and women loved the chance to get out some aggression for a good cause. The carnage was presided over by none other than the fire captain himself. We knew better than to try to sneak an extra swing on his watch—he was an usher at our church, after all, and sat behind us in the pews. My cousins and I firmly believed that he'd tell on us to Jesus if we tried.

Church is also where we pray for the safety of the men and women who put on the American uniform to protect our way of life, who fight for the cause of freedom around the world, and who remind us just how precious that freedom is. That's why they get the loudest cheers during the Fourth of July parades and why they get the best seats in the house at the fireworks show. It's the least we can do, after all they've done.

We understand this in Flyover Nation. It's why our states have some of the highest percentages of military enlistees in the country. It's why, while the people on the coasts have "better" things to do than serve their country, the men and women of Flyover Nation consistently answer the call. People like George Sisler.

George Sisler—Flyover Hero

George Kenton Sisler—who went by "Ken"—was born in 1937 in Dexter, Missouri. Dexter is a tiny town of less than eight thousand, nestled in the southeastern corner of Missouri, just a few hours from where I grew up. But Ken's desire to serve his country would end up taking him around the world.

He first joined up in 1956, serving in the Army National Guard for a year, then another year in the Army Reserves. In 1958 he enlisted in the air force, where he served until 1962.

He also found time to attend college, graduating from Arkansas State University in 1964 with a degree in education. After graduation he promptly joined the army once again, was put on the track to Officer Candidate School, and earned his commission as a second lieutenant in June of 1965.[56]

For a boy from Flyover Nation, Sisler did a lot of flying himself—literal flying through the air. Sisler liked to jump out of airplanes. He had worked as a "smoke jumper"—an airborne firefighter—in Missouri. One of his air force buddies recalled that Sisler would show home movies of himself "parachuting into forest fires that he had taken from a helmet mounted movie camera"—and this was decades before the days of GoPro![57]

He was also a competitive parachutist in college, and a fearless one at that. An unfortunately timed injury forced Sisler to wear a cast on one leg on the eve of the 1963 National Collegiate Skydiving Championship. But Ken jumped anyway, cast and all, and took home the top prize.[58]

The army clearly recognized this talent and bravery. Lieutenant Sisler joined the Special Forces—the Green Berets—and was assigned as an intelligence officer to the Headquarters Company, Fifth Special Forces Group (Airborne) serving in Vietnam. That was how he found himself leading a joint patrol of American and Allied South Vietnamese troops operating in enemy territory on February 7, 1967.

Lieutenant Sisler's patrol came under attack from three sides simultaneously. A much larger enemy force had them virtually surrounded. Sisler acted quickly—he set his men up a defensive perimeter and got on the radio to report the engagement and call for air support. As he moved around the position taking stock of his men and offering encouragement, it became clear that two soldiers were still stranded, wounded, outside the perimeter. Sisler did not take the time to issue any orders—he jumped up and ran to get them himself.[59]

He found the first of the injured men and proceeded to carry him back toward their lines. This only presented a more desirable target to the enemy, who opened up with even greater firepower. Sisler knew that if he didn't act fast, neither he nor the man he was carrying stood a chance of making it. So he set down the wounded man and picked up his rifle in time to kill three enemy soldiers bearing down on them. He then threw a grenade to take out a machine-gun nest. Having cleared the way, Sisler dragged the wounded soldier back behind his own lines. But the battle was not yet over.[60]

Just as he was arriving back at his position, the enemy laid down concentrated fire on their left flank, wounding a number of Sisler's men. Seeing his line in danger of breaking, Sisler grabbed some extra grenades and charged forward from the weakened left flank himself. He shot at the advancing enemy troops and hurled multiple grenades, and the communist forces began to fall back. The official report later said: "This singularly heroic action broke up the vicious assault and forced the enemy to begin withdrawing."[61] But it was a fighting withdrawal, and as they left, the communists claimed another casualty—Lieutenant Sisler himself.

George Kenton Sisler, from Dexter, Missouri, Flyover Nation, USA, was killed in action half a world away in Vietnam on February 7, 1967. He would never jump out of another airplane. But the courage that had driven him to jump into raging infernos to help his community as a smoke jumper, the courage that had sent him flying into collegiate skydiving legend with a cast on his leg, the courage that had led him to volunteer to serve in Vietnam—that was the same courage that spurred him to leave the safety of his defensive position to rescue his comrades and repel the enemy's attack.

For his gallantry, Ken Sisler was awarded the Congressional Medal of Honor. The citation concluded: "His extraordinary leadership, infinite courage, and selfless concern for his men saved the lives of a number of his comrades. His actions reflect great credit upon himself and uphold the highest traditions of the military service."[62]

His name lives on in other ways, not just on land but at sea too. The army named a building after him—Sisler Hall—at its Intelligence Center at Fort Huachuca, Arizona, in 1988.[63] Ten years later the navy christened a vehicle transport ship the USNS *Sisler*, an act the military called "a fitting tribute to all military and civilian personnel who have played an important role in the history of military intelligence and have paid the supreme sacrifice in their service to the nation."[64]

The *Sisler* still sails the seas today—a long way from Dexter, Missouri. It carries to the far corners of the world the name of an adventurous kid from Flyover Nation, a champion skydiver who took the ultimate leap of faith by answering his country's call many times over and gave his life in the fight against communism.

The soldiers and veterans of today's global war on terror, risking their lives in places like Iraq and Afghanistan, are a new generation of heroes, heirs to the tradition of duty and honor handed down by men like Ken Sisler. And like Missouri's own Lieutenant Sisler, it would seem that most of the men and women serving in our country's armed forces today came to the services after growing up in Flyover Nation.

The consumer financial analytics site WalletHub released a survey in 2015 that covered, among other things, military service by individual state. Its results in this area were split into two major categories: the percentage of the state's residents who had enlisted in the military and the number of veterans per capita living in the state. Taking a look at the high and low ends of these lists doesn't exactly yield a lot of surprises.

According to WalletHub, which cited data from government and nonprofit sources, the state with the highest percentage of enlisted residents was Georgia. Following the Peach State came South Carolina, Florida, Alaska, and Alabama— all places elites studiously avoid, unless it's to jet to a fancy beach house in the parts of Florida set aside for tourists with money to burn.[65]

On the other side, the state with the smallest percentage of the population serving was North Dakota—definitely a Flyover state, but one currently in the midst of an energy boom. But not far from the bottom were classic coastal bastions Massachusetts and Connecticut (numbers forty-six and forty-seven, respectively). After all, who would want to risk the chance of getting deployed and missing the Harvard-Yale game?[66]

The states with the most veterans per capita can also be found squarely in Flyover Nation: Alaska tops the list, followed by Montana, Maine, Virginia, and West Virginia. The states with the fewest former service members include President Obama's current home state, Illinois, Nancy Pelosi's home state, California, and of course—rounding out the bottom of the list—New Jersey and New York. WalletHub found that Alaska had twice as many veterans per capita as New York.[67]

A look at the Department of Defense's own data on enlistment from 2013 widens the lens a bit, looking at regions instead of individual states. This is what helps make crystal clear the difference between Flyover country's contributions to our military forces and those of the more rarefied sections of the country.

According to DOD, 44 percent of recruits across all branches in 2013 came from the South. And the South is only home to 36 percent of Americans between eighteen and twenty-four years of age. By contrast, the Northeast, which holds 18 percent of all eighteen- to twenty-four-year-olds, contributed only 14 percent of new recruits into the military's ranks, making that "the most underrepresented region of the country" in the armed forces, according to *Business Insider*. *Business Insider* further confirmed that in 2013 "some of the lowest rates of state-by-state enlistment are in New England and the Northeast, Maine notwithstanding."[68] God bless those Mainers. The other New Englanders think they're crazy and only like to talk to them when they're catching lobsters for the Connecticut- and Massachusetts-registered yachts docked in Bar Harbor.

The trend goes back even further. In 2010 then–Secretary of Defense Robert Gates—a veteran of both Democratic and Republican administrations—laid out the issue in a speech at Duke University in North Carolina, itself an elite institution that draws heavily from California and New York.[69] Secretary Gates noted:

> *In this country, [the] propensity to serve is most pronounced in the South and Mountain West, and in rural areas and small towns nationwide—a propensity that well exceeds these communities' portion of the population as a whole. Concurrently, the percentage of the force from the Northeast, West Coast, and major cities continues to decline.*[70]

In effect, the young people of the South and the Mountain West are signing up to shoulder the burden of defense for the rest of the country and are particularly picking up the slack for the people of the "Northeast, West Coast, and major cities." I wouldn't expect anything less.

Yet those people are only too happy to look down on both the military itself and the "redneck flyover folks" who fill its ranks. They see the military as fit only for loser high school dropouts (in fact, enlisted military personnel were found to be "significantly more likely to have a high school education than their peers").[71] Of course, coastal elites have no problem entrusting the defense of the nation to these people they despise, so long as it leaves them free to concentrate on the pressing business of negotiating leveraged corporate buyouts and organizing tennis parties.

Simply put, the elitist snots don't want to serve, so they don't do it. According to Kathy Roth-Doquet, who cowrote *AWOL: The Unexcused Absence of America's Upper Classes from Military Service and How It Hurts Our Country*, less than 1 percent of Ivy League graduates enter the service. She points out that while previous generations of elites—including the Kennedy and Bush political dynasties and the Sulzbergers of *New York Times* fame—signed up to do their duty, today's elites aren't even giving it a thought. Why? Roth-Doquet suggests that "narrow self-interest, a sense of other priorities or a misguided sense of moral preference means most of the upper class never considers military service."[72]

This bodes well for the nation, doesn't it? The progeny of the people who are supposed to be running the show blow off any sense of duty to their country because of self-interest, "other priorities," or "moral preference." The last of these just might be the most sickening. It is yet another example of that classic elitist tendency to try to dictate the moral compass of the rest of the country, to make all of us rubes follow their version of "San Francisco values."

Roth-Doquet takes a guess at the source of elites' "moral" distaste for military service. "In my own travels to talk about this issue," she writes, "the most problematic comment I've come across is an idea expressed by many, including many in the upper classes, that it is somehow more moral to refrain from military service than to serve, because that way one can avoid an 'immoral' war."[73]

If you listen closely to coastals talk, you start to realize they perform a kind of sacrifice sleight of hand. Every politician talks about making sacrifices for one's fellow countrymen. But if you look at the details, you realize we're often talking about two very different things. When someone enlists, he or she is going down a much more difficult life path in order to protect the people he or she knows and loves. In Flyover we know how to volunteer for a lot of sacrifices: for our families, for our God, for our neighbors, and for everyone standing along that parade route at Freedom Fest. But when the coastals talk about sacrifice, they usually mean forcing you to give up money for someone else somewhere who is never going to show up to a parade to honor you.

When you hear a coastal put their hand over their heart and say "sacrifice," you can bet the other hand is going into your pocketbook.

Those who make the choice to serve do not have the luxury of cherry-picking the conflicts in which they engage. That's not how the military works. It's about defending the country, not about the finer points of political arguments. As Roth-Doquet points out, it's not political at all: "The oath given at the 'pinning on' ceremony for a second lieutenant or a general involves not a promise to fight a particular war or support a given president but to protect and defend the Constitution."[74] That being the case, what is the true "moral preference" of the elites? Do they simply not think the country—which has clearly given them so much—is worth defending?

I would like to pose that question to a young Ivy League graduate of today—assuming, of course, he or she is not one of the minuscule number who see fit to serve. I'd also like to ask them just what their priorities are. If military service is so distasteful, what would they rather do? Go out to the western desert and weave baskets and "find themselves"? Or on the other extreme, maybe they'd rather make a beeline for Wall Street and join a hedge fund or investment bank. They've got to find something to do until the trust fund kicks in, so why not join the crony capitalist express? I guess they don't have a "moral preference" against making piles of money off subprime mortgages while Flyover folks end up losing their homes. At least the elites can always rely on the kids from Flyover Nation to fill the ranks of the military and make the world safe for corporate raiding.

Secretary Gates speculated in 2010 that "the military's own basing and recruiting decisions" were a major factor, leading to heavy recruitment from areas with a significant military presence and among individuals "whose friends, classmates, and parents have already served."[75] A Defense Department spokesman took a similar line in 2014, telling *Business Insider* that "one reason might be exposure to large military bases in states where there are higher enlistment rates."[76] Promilitary areas produce more recruits, who then go on to serve and live on bases in promilitary areas, and the cycle repeats. This idea has been expressed by, among others, Benjamin Luxenberg—who managed to breach the elite confines of Harvard and Brandeis *and* serve in the Marine Corps—who observed that "inadvertently, America is forging a military caste, separate from the larger electorate and distinct from its future leaders."[77]

It's not hard to see that America's elites and the military personnel who keep the country safe for them—and for all of us—are worlds apart. I know which group I'd rather spend time with any day of the week. But it can't all be chalked up to the location of military bases and the freedom-loving pockets of the population centered on them. It's about values too. Flyover Nation doesn't send more recruits into the service just because it already has some bases there—it's also because people who grew up in that environment understand the value of service. They appreciate what America has given them and choose to put their lives on the line in order to repay that debt.

When you're already insulated by layers of money and power, it's easy to lose sight of that. Deciding whether to sail to Bermuda or the Caymans this summer becomes a more pressing priority. But for the substantial percentage of members of the military who hail from Flyover Nation, the choice is very simple: It's about duty, honor, and service.

A 2008 deep dive into the demographics of the military by the Heritage Foundation included a good look at the makeup of the American servicemen that can't be gleaned from data alone: "A soldier's demographic characteristics are of little importance in the military, which values honor, leadership, self-sacrifice, courage, and integrity—qualities that cannot be quantified."[78] It's true—those cannot be quantified. But in Flyover Nation we know them when we see them. And we see them an awful lot. One of the biggest drivers of the disconnect between the military and the rest of the country transcends regional differences and goes straight to the top. It should come as no surprise that the root of this problem is found in Washington, DC, among our political elites. In this rarefied group, the percentage of veterans is at its lowest level in decades.

There was once a time when military service was almost a prerequisite for election to the House of Representatives, the Senate, or the presidency. The Democrats understood this just as well as the Republicans. John F. Kennedy was a decorated war hero, and Jimmy Carter, who graduated from the U.S. Naval Academy just after World War II, served in nuclear submarines. Daniel Inouye, a Democratic senator from Hawaii, earned the Congressional Medal of Honor serving with a Japanese American unit during World War II, losing an arm in the process. His fellow Democrat Max Cleland of Georgia lost an arm and both legs in Vietnam.

Now, among both Democrats and Republicans, the number of veterans serving in the legislative branch of the government has plummeted. Sadly, there are only one fourth as many veterans serving today as there were in the wake of the Vietnam War. In 1976, 77 percent of all senators and House members had previously served in the military, according to American Legion data. In 2014, the Legion and the House Armed Services Committee calculated that that number had dropped to 20 percent.[79]

When the 113th Congress began its first session in January 2013, there were eighty-nine veterans in the House and nineteen in the Senate, so Congress still maintains some heroes among its ranks.[80] Texas representative Sam Johnson and Arizona senator

John McCain were both decorated pilots—Johnson in the air force and McCain in the navy—and were both held prisoner by the North Vietnamese for extended periods. But those ranks are thinning. New Jersey Democratic senator Frank Lautenberg, the last World War II veteran in the Senate, died in 2013. The following year the House lost its last two WWII vets—Democrat John Dingell of Michigan retired and Republican Ralph Hall of Texas lost a primary election. Dingell closed his career in public life at the age of eighty-eight, and Hall was ninety-one. We desperately need more veterans in elected office.

It's not just members of Congress themselves who are increasingly discharging their duties without the benefit of military service. Their children, part of the next generation of elites, seemingly want nothing to do with the armed forces either. Just 1 percent of all federal legislators have a child in the service, according to Kathy Roth-Doquet in *AWOL*. And as she points out, "the Capitol building is no different from other places where the leadership class in this country gathers—no different from the boardrooms, newsrooms, ivory towers and penthouses of our nation."[81] This doesn't just mean that Congress as an institution has less of an idea about the realities of war. It also weakens the patriotism of the entire body. The further removed Congress—and other elites—are from our military, the more they risk losing sight of what it is our servicemen and servicewomen are fighting for, what exactly makes America great.

Some might call this "American exceptionalism." This is the idea that the United States of America is somehow special, different from any other nation on earth. This is not a new idea. Alexis de Tocqueville first described it. Writing in his report on a visit to the relatively new United States in the early nineteenth century called *Democracy in America*, he stated, "The position of the Americans is therefore quite exceptional."[82]

Former Speaker of the House Newt Gingrich explains that our unique founding is the basis for this exceptionalism:

> *The ideals expressed in the Declaration of Independence, and the unique American identity that arose from an American civilization that honored them, form what we call today "American Exceptionalism."*[83]

Gingrich is absolutely right. No other country came into being like ours did. Our founding documents have guided the nation from the beginning and continue to guide us today. The Declaration of Independence set us on a course and the Constitution forms the bedrock of our system of government. The first ten amendments, the Bill of Rights, set in stone the freedoms guaranteed to every American. If staying committed to those freedoms, guarding them vigilantly, and being ready and willing to defend them by any means necessary is part of being "exceptional," I'll take it.

Not surprisingly, this idea attracts plenty of criticism, even in the United States. The leftist academic Howard Zinn, for instance, has praised the "growing refusal to accept U.S. domination and the idea of American exceptionalism" and proclaimed, "The true heroes of our history are those Americans who refused to accept that we have a special claim to morality and the right to exert our force on the rest of the world."[84]

As if all that made America exceptional was "exerting force" on other countries. Obviously there's no pleasing the professional Left.

But one person, no matter what their political persuasion, should be able to accept that the United States is special, especially if they intend to lead that nation—right? Presidents of the United States are politicians, sure, and their positions will be different from other politicians'. But anyone who wants to be president should be able to agree that the country they want to lead is exceptional . . . shouldn't they?

Not if that president is Barack Hussein Obama II. His view of how exceptional his country is is just a little bit . . . different. He would probably call it "nuanced." It could also be called "cowardly." Here's the Obama definition of "American exceptionalism": "I believe in American exceptionalism, just as I suspect that the Brits believe in British exceptionalism and the Greeks believe in Greek exceptionalism."[85]

The wording of this statement Obama made in April 2009, just months after taking office, raises the question: If every country thinks of itself as "exceptional," how truly exceptional can any one nation be? It's as though, in Obama's view, the "exceptional" label is to be handed out like participation trophies at a kids' soccer game or free cars at an Oprah taping. I'm exceptional! You're exceptional! The whole world is exceptional! Kumbaya, you guys!

That comment generated a lot of criticism, and rightly so, as people questioned how this man they'd just elected really felt about his country's place in the world. Since then, Obama has made plenty of statements with stronger wording, like his declaring, "I believe in American exceptionalism with every fiber of my being," at West Point in 2014.[86] Though his actions are more consistent with his earlier, unvarnished pronouncement. A leader who thinks of his nation as truly exceptional does not base his foreign policy on the idea of "leading from behind."

But we saw signs of this. It's not like it was a surprise. The language was there when Obama was just a first-term senator making his "audacious" run for the presidency. In July 2008 he lectured to an audience in Powder Springs, Georgia, about the need for Americans to be more worldly, starting from a young age. "Instead of worrying about whether immigrants can learn English—they'll learn English—you need to make sure your child can speak Spanish." He went on to detail his "embarrassment" in the face of multilingual European tourists:

> *It's embarrassing when Europeans come over here, they all speak English, they speak French, they speak German. And then we go over to Europe and all we can say is merci beaucoup.*[87]

Sometimes it feels like Obama has based his entire presidency on this kind of "embarrassment" by his uncultured fellow Americans. We're not exceptional—we're embarrassing because we don't speak enough languages.

Also during the 2008 campaign, Obama mocked "bitter" voters in "small towns in Pennsylvania" and "a lot of small towns in the Midwest" who "cling to guns or religion or antipathy toward people who aren't like them or anti-immigrant sentiment or anti-trade sentiment as a way to explain their frustrations."[88] The best part? He was speaking to a room full of donors in San Francisco. That must be how you explain Flyover Nation to Bay Area elites.

Shortly before the election, Obama told a crowd in Missouri: "We are five days away from fundamentally transforming the United States of America."[89] Apparently this didn't raise enough red flags in the next five days. But the message seems clear—if you love your country, especially if you find it "exceptional," why exactly is your goal to "fundamentally transform" it?

It's not just Barack Obama who seems to feel less than patriotic about this country. It's a family affair, with his wife, lunch czar Michelle, getting into the act as well. This is the woman who notably announced—not once but twice, at two different campaign rallies in Wisconsin in 2008: "For the first time in my adult life I am proud of my country."[90] Elsewhere on the campaign trail she echoed her husband's call for transformative change:

> *We are going to have to change our conversation; we're going to have to change our traditions, our history; we're going to have to move into a different place as a nation.*[91]

It looks like one of the traditions she aimed to change was respect for our nation's most prominent symbol. In 2011, during a 9/11 commemoration ceremony, she turned to her husband and muttered something that looked—to people reading her lips—a lot like "All this—for a flag?"[92] She then shook her head, and her husband nodded.

America is an exceptional nation, and our leaders need to appreciate that. Patriotic leadership is essential for maintaining this country's place in the world. This is the kind of patriotism you see in the young men and women—most of whom come from Flyover Nation—who make the decision to serve their country in the armed forces. You see it in the celebrations that take place in Middle America every Fourth of July, as communities come together to celebrate with pride the country they love. Elites like Barack and Michelle Obama consider it uncultured to be patriotic—why celebrate being an American when you can be a multilingual citizen of the world? That's why they dismiss anyone who doesn't think like them as a "bitter" malcontent who "clings to guns or religion"—because, of course, only bitter people would be driven to own a gun or go to church.

They'll never understand Flyover Nation, and frankly, we're just fine with that.

Perhaps the real divide over the military comes from the coastals' fear of guns and the people who know how to use them.

So what is it about guns that coastals just can't seem to understand?

CHAPTER 5

A Heart Problem and a Criminal-Justice Problem

For years whenever I stayed the night at my grandparents' tiny house in the Ozarks on the other side of an abandoned mine, I slept a foot away from an unlocked gun cabinet stocked with all sorts of rifles and pistols. Grandpa kept a full rack of rifles mounted on the rear glass of his truck. Everyone carried. All us kids had BB guns and spent countless summer afternoons lining up little green army men on Grandma and Grandpa's picnic table to shoot down one by one. Yet in all of those years, with all of us grandkids running around, nothing bad ever happened. Before I was old enough to understand or fear the serious consequences of unquenched curiosity coupled with a disrespect for private property, I feared punishment by my mother. My mother's face physically resembles that of an eagle's when angry: pointed, beady eyes, lips pursed into a beak. It's positively terrifying. I think even more than that, I was afraid to disappoint my grandparents. All of us felt that way. When Grandma or Grandpa told you something certain, you did it, you followed it. I couldn't imagine disrespecting my grandparents by going through their things, opening the handmade gun cabinet that my uncle had made for Grandpa, and taking something that wasn't mine to take. My mother kept a loaded .38 in her nightstand. I knew it was there—I'd seen it before—but I never would have imagined opening that drawer and taking it.

When I was in fifth or sixth grade I heard a story about a kid who was playing at a friend's house and the pair had the idea to go through the parents' drawers because the son knew his dad kept a gun somewhere. They found it, they played with it, and one of them was shot and killed. My first thought was horror, as in *Why* did they think it was a toy? My second thought was *Where did they get the idea that it was okay to rifle through other people's belongings?* It was a tragedy, but how did my grandparents, who were armed to the teeth with guns all over the house, help raise twenty-eight grandkids, have a house crawling with children and adults, and never have a single theft or accident? Mind you, it wasn't just my grandparents; it was the *entire town* in which they lived. Everyone lived like that and still does. It's just how it is, and to this day there hasn't been such an incident.

People on the coasts think that the Second Amendment is nothing but a codified exception for hunting meant only to apply to muskets. It's not. As I wrote in my previous book, the founders were made aware of emerging firearms technology when John Belton wrote to the Continental Congress and informed them that he had, in fact, created the very first automatic rifle, to the enemy's "immortal sorrow."[93] Congress considered buying

Belton's guns for the Continental Army, but all consideration ceased when they could not navigate around the immense cost of Belton's gun. They didn't ban Belton from manufacturing such weaponry, however; they didn't force him to supply the Continental Army, either. Here John Belton (and others, like James Puckle) clearly demonstrated that he had weapons technology that was superior in rate of fire, and it wasn't banned or regulated. The idea that the founders meant only muskets when drafting the Second Amendment should embarrass any historical illiterate who makes the argument. Those people should be publicly mocked, as anyone making such an argument is outing themselves as a historical illiterate. The "musket argument" is the same as arguing that speech made via a printing press is somehow less protected than that made by a quill. The innovation and technological development that brought us from the musket to where we are today didn't come from the government; it came from the private sector, from average, everyday Americans who saw a need for firearm improvement and wanted to fill it. There exist many firearms manufacturers that are small, humble, mom-and-pop operations. Black Rain Ordnance from southern Missouri, Kel-Tec in Florida, Black Swamp Firearms in Michigan, Nemesis Arms in Kentucky, and Aklys Defense in Louisiana are all small businesses providing jobs in their communities while expanding on the current platform of firearms by improving function, modernizing form, and inventing new ways to exercise the Second Amendment. These aren't big manufacturers, and even if they were, every big manufacturer started as a small one and blossomed into a success story. Smith & Wesson began humbly as a shop run by Horace Smith and Daniel Wesson; Samuel Colt was the son of a farmer and became an indentured worker at the age of eleven. As the needs of Americans progressed from the Civil War to the American frontier, so did their needs for arms, which these privately owned businesses fulfilled.

As I covered in my previous book, *Hands Off My Gun*, no part of the United States is exempt from criminal activity, but the areas where there exists a higher rate of homicide by firearm are areas where there is a breakdown of criminal penalty, increased restrictions on firearms, and an increase in gang activity. The gun homicide rate is driven by repeat offenders[94] who illegally use illegally possessed firearms. It's not driven by farmers, ranchers, stay-at-home moms, and the like in Flyover.

As a side note, be wary of any gun-death statistics waved at you, as the antigun lobby always includes justified shootings (police who take down bad guys) and suicides in the total number. The vast majority of gun deaths in America are self-inflicted. Those people are not taking their own lives with the kind of firearms coastals get worked up about. But you don't hear them worrying instead about a suicide epidemic, as they're too busy trying to let physicians bring the suicide numbers up nationwide.

Coastals also like to point out that Flyover has more guns, so it has more gun deaths. And that's true, but not because we're killing each other. Homicide is much more common in the cities.

I wrote in *Hands Off My Gun* about how I grew up with firearms. During the Fourth of July in Flyover Nation, when there is a momentary lull between small cannon and bottle rockets, you can hear gunfire in the distance. People in Flyover like to exercise their Second Amendment rights as part of the Independence Day festivities. My family didn't teach *just* about firearms and firearm safety; they taught *three other things* as part of that lesson: respect for life, respect for private property, and to treat one another with love. They're biblical lessons absent today because the ever-growing secular world has a problem with God. As a kid, before getting to the playing-with-a-gun party, I'd have had to bypass *respect for private property*. We have a problem with "Thou shalt not covet" in today's society. Just because you see something doesn't mean it's yours to take. We also have a problem with *respecting life* in this country. I can't imagine the difficulty children today have with this concept, considering that special-interest groups preach to them from infancy that they're dispensable and that if they ever want to have a child, that child is dispensable too—just stop in to your local Planned Parenthood as your trusty source of postconception birth control. So many in Flyover scratch their heads at the contradiction posed by so many who claim to want to "save just one life" when discussing reducing crimes committed with illegally used firearms, as these are the *exact same people* who have no problem with a Planned Parenthood on every corner in urban America.

The sad fact of the matter is that it's become politically incorrect, be it in foreign policy (which has affected domestic policy and the way we respond to and handle terror here) or criminal-justice policy, to state the obvious and enforce existing law. We're told to rehabilitate instead of punish and falsely believe that grace and justice can't exist together.

On December 2, 2015, two terrorists walked into the Inland Regional Center and opened fire, killing fourteen and wounding more. One of the terrorists, a foreigner from Pakistan named Tashfeen Malik, had a diabolical unibrow and had ranted for years in private social media messages about jihad, but Jeh Johnson's Department of Homeland Security isn't even allowed to take *public* messages into consideration when granting visas because, says a former senior department official, Johnson fears "bad public relations" and a civil-liberties backlash.[95] Yes, far worse things than the backlash Johnson is facing after the deaths of fourteen Americans because Johnson was worried about his own backside. I'm sure the families of those fourteen victims found solace in Johnson's dutiful devotion to political correctness. The terrorists had pledged allegiance to ISIS online before the attacks and meticulously mapped out their strategy, but they were as good at building bombs as Ahmed Mohamed, the clock boy, was at repurposing clock guts into a pencil case and calling it his own invented IED clock. Neighbors saw young Middle Eastern men coming to and going from Tashfeen Malik and Syed Farook's home, and the two had turned their garage into an IED factory, but no one said anything because neighbors didn't want anyone to think that they were racially profiling.

Political correctness is killing people.

Instead of focusing on the lax vetting process for visa seekers like Malik, Democrats immediately blamed the Second Amendment. Guns, not terror, were the culprit. Upon finally admitting that it *was* an act of terror, the president gave an address where he intoned that we shouldn't judge all Muslims based on these two terrorists (or the one from Oklahoma, or Garland, or Chattanooga, or Boston, or the Underwear Bomber, or the attempted Times Square bomber, or the 9/11 hijackers, or the USS *Cole* bombers, or the Benghazi attackers, or the Beltway snipers—I could continue at length) but should by all means judge all law-abiding gun owners based on the weapons that these two terrorists illegally used—and were in illegal possession of: The rifles were not obtained through a legal transfer and were modified to the point of criminality in California, which boasts the strictest of the "expanded background checks" that Democrats admire. Our existing laws criminalizing murder would have prevented the attack, to say nothing of our existing gun laws, if passing laws were all that fighting terrorism required.

I was on air when the terrorist attack happened, and even with the name "Syed Farook" making the rounds on scanners, it was too early to call a motive until confirmed by law enforcement, but what we have learned over the past two years is that you can't count on the administration to name motives when the motive is Islamic terror. The administration flirted with repeating its Fort Hood travesty in calling the San B~~~~~dino attack "workplace violence," even as law enforceme telligence departments knew without a doubt that t act of terror. They would do this again with anoth attack, the first of 2016. On the evening of January man in a long white robe fired a stolen pistol ir cruiser, seriously wounding Officer Jesse Hartnett suspect, identified as Edward Archer, had pledged his allegiance to ISIS and said that he had "tried to execute" the officer "in the name of Islam."[96] Democratic mayor Jim Kenney blamed guns and said, "There are too many guns on the street."[97] Funny thing about that: Archer used a gun he had stolen from a cop in 2013. Oops. Kenney was clearly shocked that an ISIS terrorist didn't submit to a background check for that stolen gun. What's more, Archer *should* have been in jail serving a ten-year sentence for a felony gun conviction in 2012. According to court documents, Archer's sentence was reduced:

Archer was sentenced to nine to 13 months in prison, was allowed to count time served and was immediately paroled. Records show he was originally arrested April 14, 2013 and was released April 30, 2013 after posting partial bail. [98]

This is a deadly judicial pattern.

In November 2015 Jalita Johnson was sentenced to only 180 days of house arrest and one year of probation for straw-purchasing a gun for her boyfriend, Marcus Wheeler (a convicted felon who told her what to buy and gave her the money to buy it), who shot and killed wife, new mom of three Officer Kerrie Orozco in Omaha earlier that same year as she and the gang task force tried to serve a warrant. The judge who handed down Johnson's wrist slap was Eleanor L. Ross, nominated by President Obama to the position in December of 2013.

In the fall of 2014, St. Louis teenager VonDerrit Myers, eighteen, was shot and killed after firing an illegally possessed gun at an off-duty officer in the Shaw neighborhood, mere blocks from my old house. Myers was up on a felony gun charge from an incident months prior but was released after Associate Circuit Court Judge Theresa Burke, in an unusual move, reduced his bond from thirty thousand dollars to one thousand (it was ten thousand, but Burke allowed Myers to pay only 10 percent for freedom).[99] Myers was ordered to wear a GPS ankle device, not leave his home except for work, school, or court, and abide by a curfew. Shockingly, as most criminals are wont to do, Myers didn't abide by these and ended up getting killed after firing at a cop while running around the neighborhood illegally possessing yet another gun. After this St. Louis mayor Francis Slay bizarrely blamed the city's violence (driven by gangs and drugs) on the Second Amendment.

"Lax gun laws in the state make it painfully easy to get a gun, carry a gun and get off on charges when someone is arrested with a gun," Slay said.[100] Yes, because VonDerrit Myers was able to legally purchase a handgun as a convicted felon under the age of twenty-one years. Please.

The problem isn't the Second Amendment; the problem is that there is no fear of criminal penalty because ridiculous judges have made such a deterrent irrelevant by reducing it to nothing. In 2010 there were eighty thousand falsifications on 4473, the form law-abiding Americans fill out and submit to the NICS, the criminal background-check system created by the NRA (in exchange for a five-day waiting period that Clinton and his Democrats wanted in the nineties). Lying on a 4473 is a felony, yet in the year mentioned, only forty-four of those were even prosecuted. Vice President Joe Biden once addressed this on a phone call noted by the *Daily Caller*:[101] Jim Baker, the NRA representative present at the meeting, recalled the vice president's words during an interview with the *Daily Caller*: "And to your point, Mr. Baker, regarding the lack of prosecutions on lying on Form 4473s, we simply don't have the time or manpower to prosecute everybody who lies on a form, that checks a wrong box, that answers a question inaccurately."

The president has done more to help and enable repeat offenders and gangbangers than he has victims or law-abiding Americans. Take, for instance, the fact that the "expanded background checks" for which he calls already existed in California, Colorado, Oregon, Washington, states where tragedies occurred in 2015. Those states had the gun restrictions that the president and anti–Second Amendment advocates wanted, yet those restrictions did nothing to prevent the criminal activity that ended up taking lives.

During the first week of January 2016, the president issued a number of executive orders, none of which would have prevented or will prevent a single tragedy from occurring because they are entirely predicated upon criminals agreeing to follow laws. The president hosted a carefully orchestrated town hall hosted by CNN, in which he rambled and monologued his way through answers to tough questions posed by Taya Kyle, Sheriff Paul Babeu, and Kimberly Corban, a rape survivor against gun control. The president even told Corban, who appeared on my radio program the following day, that she shouldn't have guns in her house, as they might cause an accident since she's the mother of young children. It was awkward and demonstrated the president's completely absence of understanding or education about firearm statistics, knowledge, and current law.

When the president stated that there should be laws regulating Internet purchases and suggested that anyone could go online and buy a gun, Flyover erupted. A family member from southern Missouri who rarely posts verbiage beyond gifs and memes, penned a caps-lock rant asking, "How stupid does the President think we are?" I was deluged with e-mails, Twitter responses, Facebook comments, messages, and phone calls from hundreds of Americans detailing exactly how they purchase their firearms. Despite the president's prime-time propaganda, no, one cannot go online and buy a gun and have it Amazon-droned to their house. All firearm purchases made online must go through an FFL, a federal firearms licensee, and a background check must be completed before the transaction is considered finished. A non-FFL may not ship a firearm to another non-FFL, anyone, anywhere, no matter what. Arrangements may be made online for a non-FFL to purchase from either an FFL or a non-FFL, so long as (1) the transaction is completed in state, and, most important, (2) the purchaser is not a prohibited possessor (prohibited from legally possessing a firearm in their state of residence; VonDerrit Myers and Marcus Wheeler are examples of prohibited possessors) and the seller is confident that the purchaser is legally allowed to purchase and carry in their state of residence. Both of these things are required by the federal law. There is no "loophole." If you are a felon or a prohibited possessor and you purchase or carry a gun anyway, **that is not a loophole. That is a criminal act.** In much the same way as if you continue to drive a car on a suspended license, you are **committing a criminal act. Breaking the law is not a "loophole."**

Yet time and time again the president and his acolytes try to convince you otherwise.

The problem isn't guns. Our country has a heart problem and a criminal-justice problem. We also don't trust the president when he tells us that he doesn't want to grab guns. I can imagine him promising us, "If you like your gun, you can keep it." Americans aren't stupid. For the past several years Obama has praised Australia's approach to gun control, which was outright confiscation (although now they're enjoying a lowered crime rate while coincidentally private firearm ownership has risen back to pre-ban 1996 levels). When the president praises confiscation, how can you believe him when he says he doesn't want to replicate that here? Americans don't believe the president on either of these matters, nor do they place confidence in him where it concerns his number one job: protection of the citizenry.

The administration assured us that ISIS was "contained." It

said people seeking amnesty, refugee status, or visas were "thoroughly vetted." The federal government has but *one* all-important job: to keep us safe. They can't do it, and a faction of them are working hard to make sure *you* can't do it, either. In the immediate aftermath of the San Bernardino attack, Dianne Feinstein and Joe Manchin, Senate Democrats, introduced proposals to restrict Second Amendment rights . . . and Fifth Amendment rights too. The Senate voted both down. Via the *Washington Post*:

> *The Senate on Thursday voted down two gun control proposals put forward by Democrats in response to this week's deadly shooting in San Bernardino, Calif., in a series of votes that highlighted the intractable party divide over how to respond to gun violence.*
>
> *The Senate rejected a measure from Sen. Joe Manchin (D-W.Va.) to expand background checks for guns purchased online and at gun shows on a 48 to 50 vote and an amendment from Sen. Dianne Feinstein (D-Calif.) to prevent individuals on the terror watch list from purchasing firearms on a 45 to 54 vote. The amendments were offered to an Obamacare repeal package currently being debated in the Senate and they needed 60 votes to be adopted.[102]*

Two things:

1. *Background checks already exist for purchases made online. Newsflash to Manchin: When you purchase guns online, they aren't shipped to your house[103] like an Amazon delivery. They must be shipped to an*

FFL, *where you then go, fill out a 4473, and get your background check, and if you're cleared you can take it home. Period. This law already exists.*

2. *If Democrats want to stop suspected terrorists placed on a watch list from buying firearms, they need to indict them. They must bring formal charges. We don't suspend the Fifth Amendment rights of due process for American citizens based on (often faulty) suspicion. There are American citizens on this list, a sizable number of whom are innocent and are mistakenly listed. We don't deny them the opportunity to have a fair trial, to face their accuser and defend themselves. A simple federal charge is enough to temporarily render them a prohibited possessor, at which time evidence will either exonerate or convict them. People like Teddy Kennedy, Representative John Lewis, Nelson Mandela, journalists Leland Vittert and Stephen Hayes, and author J. Christian Adams were all listed. My Vietnam-veteran uncle was temporarily placed on such a list at one time. Between the time he retired and when he passed away (in 2015), he had three hobbies: muscle cars, covered bridges (he was a member of a covered-bridge society and went about the country photographing them), and traveling the world. He raised government suspicion once because he ventured to Iceland to sightsee; a couple of weeks later he tried to fly himself and my aunt to Hawaii for a little R&R but was barred from boarding. My aunt recalled that it was some time before he was finally allowed to travel normally again.*

> *Stripping someone of a natural right based on suspicion alone is a penalty without a conviction. There is no disclosure as to how someone is included on the list. And once you're on it? It's next to impossible to get yourself removed. Democrats want inclusion on the list to count as a conviction because it excuses them from bringing formal charges based on evidence. If you have evidence, bring charges. This expectation that the American people should bear the burden of the state's inability, or outright refusal, to prosecute suspected terrorists isn't constitutional. It's difficult to believe that Democrats are serious about barring terrorists from owning firearms when they've armed them and seemingly refuse to prosecute. Democrats want to sell you the emergency of barring terrorist access to firearms while ignoring the very law that would allow them to do so while avoiding infringing Second Amendment rights. They cannot combat terrorism unless they are given consent to list anyone—and considering how zealously they placed returning veterans[104] and tea partiers[105] on terror watch lists a few years ago, you should be concerned.*

These Democrats are falling victim to the Law of Bureaucratic Reproduction. More government always leads to even more government. If you ask the people who make red tape what the solution to a problem is, they will always answer, "More red tape." The trouble is you can't kill ISIS with paperwork, though you'd be surprised how many small businesses you can lay to rest with it.

So many people on the coasts are far removed from the reality of existence as faced by many in Flyover. They don't harvest their own meat, rely on their own effort to raise produce, or depend upon their conservation habits to keep food production sustainable, nor do they rely on themselves for their own protection. In Flyover police aren't as many as they are in highly concentrated urban coastal areas. My family members like to say they carry a gun because it's easier than carrying a cop. Even cops acknowledge that they can't be present at all times, and the average 9-1-1 response time ranges between twelve and twenty minutes.[106] That's a lot of time on which to gamble the safety of you and your family.

East and West Coast denizens tend to view firearms as "tools of murder," as they so often tell me on social media and whenever I debate them on television. Here again we see the viral vampires jumping on whatever's trending on Twitter to stake out the moral cyberground while those of us in Flyover are thinking past page views and Facebook likes.

Where I come from, we view firearms as tools of defense. We're not just hopping on a headline about someone far from us. No, our perspective was shaped by knowing people who've had to rely on a gun in an emergency. In a 2013 report commissioned by President Obama, the CDC and National Research Council concluded that the "use of firearms for self-defense is an important deterrent" and noted that defensive gun use outweighs criminal usage, with DGU occurring "500,000 to more than 3 million [times] per year."[107] The study corroborated a Pew study released in October 2015 that found gun homicides are in a steady decline and have been since the nineties, that we're safer now than we've ever been, but that fewer than 12 percent of Americans realize this.[108] I would add that this is because neither the media nor the administration finds that such a reality serves their antigun agenda. This partially contributes to coastals' abhorrence of firearms. They're literally told day after day the complete opposite of the truth: that a legally well-armed society is a polite and safer society.

Contrary to the abstraction of coastal anti–Second Amendment advocates and their like-minded plants attempting to infiltrate Flyover, guns aren't murder objects; they're inanimate objects for prochoice defense. They're things that are given to us by our grandpas to signal our coming of age and used to harvest our own protein from nature. They're what our moms and dads teach us to use to defend ourselves against someone who wishes to do us evil. To us women, they're the difference between being a victim and being a survivor. I sometimes wonder if living dependent upon the company of others and in proximity to others for so long degrades and devolves our innate instinct for individualism and survival. We know that it serves to make us greater targets for terrorists who hope to inflict mass casualties. In an interview a few years ago, Ben Carson told Glenn Beck that he felt guns should be regulated according to geography, that people in urban areas might not need them as people in rural areas did. He defended that statement to me once on my radio program, saying it was "inartfully put." It's a line of reasoning I've heard before: that the fact that people live close to one another somehow makes inanimate objects more dangerous. The abolishment of reduced criminal sentences would contribute to a reduction in recidivism rates for repeat offenders, yet that solves only a portion of the problem plaguing Chicago, Baltimore, DC, and other areas with high crime rates. The other problem is a breakdown of society. A dissolution of morality, of law and order, of respect for life and property, things most of us were taught from a young age. We glorify violence in film while punishing children on the playground if they reimagine the epic battle of good versus evil in a game of cops and robbers. We lecture people about valuing life after a gangbanger shoots a kid in Chicago while others defend Planned Parenthood harvesting infant body parts and selling them for profit.

Every time I appear on television some faceless male progressive troll or female free-birth-control advocate refers to me as a "gun humper" or "NRA prostitute." Their pejoratives betray their "equality" shtick as they seek to sexually degrade and demean any woman who disagrees with them on the issue of firearms—and the manner in which they always equate firearms and phalluses also serves as an insight into their psyche. (I'd say it's those men and women who have an unhealthy view of firearms and sex, not truly empowered, Second Amendment–supporting women.) Women comprise the fastest-growing demographic in the firearms industry, and more and more women are participating in shooting sports and hunting. Entire organizations (the Well Armed Woman, for instance) are springing up around the country to accommodate the growing demand for female fellowship. As I've said before, women had the right to bear arms before we had the right to vote, and there isn't an anti–Second Amendment advocate who's going to persuade an empowered, knowledgeable, Second Amendment–supporting woman to give up one of her natural rights to satisfy the emotionally based, non-fact-based propaganda they peddle. Definitely not in Flyover Nation.

We need a reformation, but not where it concerns gun rights.

It's easy to spark criminal-justice reform but not so much to spark a reformation of the nation's heart. That requires people leaving their comfort zones and effecting change themselves. It requires the sacrifice of personal time, expense, and even comfort. Not many are willing to do so, and the current economy makes it even harder. Yet in spite of these obstacles, we must try. This is where the coasts would be wise to pattern themselves after Flyover, where the values that built America still exist.

When we don't do it right, a whole city can go up in flames, as one did a year and a half ago.

CHAPTER 6

Professional Agitators

It was November 25, 2014, and Missouri was burning.

The town of Ferguson, not far from where I used to live, was the scene of violent protests that quickly escalated into looting and arson in the wake of the decision by a grand jury not to file criminal charges against local police officer Darren Wilson in the shooting death of eighteen-year-old Michael Brown the previous August. There had been protests then too, in the hot summer days that followed Brown's death. People from all over the country and the world had descended on this little corner of the Flyover Nation, about thirty miles from my hometown, to protest what they firmly believed was an unjust killing motivated by racism on the part of Officer Wilson. They burned down the QuikTrip, a family barbecue joint, and a beauty salon and looted a liquor store, among many others. Obtaining justice for Mike Brown apparently involved burning down black-owned businesses and stealing beer.

The mood of the city grew violent. As the crowds camped out in front of the Ferguson police station and elsewhere in town, waiting for news of the grand jury's decision, the tension ratcheted up to new levels. The grand jury had met over several months, hearing from witnesses and reviewing documents related to Brown's death to separate the facts of the case from the many fictions ("Hands up, don't shoot" being one) that spread through the media. But the protesters' only idea of justice was an indictment—Wilson's head on a legal platter. When the announcement came down that the grand jury had declined to indict the officer, Ferguson exploded.

"Burn this motherf**ker down!" Louis Head, Brown's stepfather, screamed to the crowd. The crowd obliged. (Head was later investigated for possibly inciting a riot.)

Rioters took to the streets. They were met with a large police presence and some in the crowd began to pelt officers with rocks and fireworks. Gunshots rang out. A car fire raged near the police station. Police used tear gas to break up the larger mobs of protesters, and as they dispersed, smaller gangs went on sprees of looting and mayhem. Two people from my flagship radio station, there covering the protests, were attacked and robbed. Near the police station, a beauty shop and a cell phone store were raided. Down the road, several businesses were set on fire, including a Walgreens and a Little Caesars pizza joint.

Across town, closer to the spot where Michael Brown was killed, the damage was worse. Along West Florissant Avenue, more businesses were torched, including a storage facility and a used car lot. Ferguson Market & Liquor, from which Brown had stolen some cigars before Wilson stopped him, was looted.

By the next afternoon, a total of twenty-one fires had been set around town and more than a dozen businesses burned.

Firefighters found themselves prevented from responding to calls at some locations because of "gunfire and objects being thrown all around," according to the *New York Times*.[109] At least 150 gunshots were reported. Police made more than sixty arrests, and fourteen people were injured.[110] During the months-long unrest, twenty-year-old Deandre Joshua lost his life. His body, burned and with a bullet wound to the head, was found in his car close to the spot where Brown had been killed in August. His death came shortly after testifying to a grand jury in Brown's case. In addition to the tragic fatality and injuries, one estimate put the physical damage from the riots after the grand jury decision at around $28 million. A British newspaper called it the worst unrest in America since the Los Angeles riots in 1992.

I watched the coverage and prayed for the safety of my friends and family in the Ferguson area. But I was also nagged by one persistent question: Why?

Other questions soon followed: Why was this town burning? Why had our news coverage been saturated for months with frantic updates as the Ferguson grand jury deliberated? Why were other protests springing up all across the country at the same time? And for that matter, who had started the whole thing? Of course, all of the attention was focused on the deadly confrontation between Wilson and Brown, but what had caused this to balloon from a local police matter to an international news story and a major "moment" in the history of race relations in America?

The answer to that question is not found in Ferguson.

The literal and figurative firestorm that swept the St. Louis area in the wake of Michael Brown's death, and continues to sweep the nation as the Black Lives Matter movement shouts its way through political rallies, college campuses, and elsewhere, is part of the long saga of betrayal of Flyover Nation by urban and coastal elites.

On the ground, trouble began with protesters from outside the area, anarchism tourists who descended on Ferguson to take advantage of the tense and at times seemingly lawless situation. Some came from St. Louis, others arrived from different parts of the city, the county, and others from different states altogether. Many were paid to protest, and when they didn't receive their checks for professional unrest, they protested that too.[111] One especially classy county resident named Bassem Masri taunted police officers on camera with such classic civil disobedience lines as: "Coward straight pig out here, b**ch! You gotta go. Your life is in danger, homie." He also offered threats, like "What happens when we take your gun?"[112]

That's a long way from "We shall overcome."

But far bigger than any street-level provocateur are the professional race-baiters who make it their mission to stir up these controversies at the national level. The moment they catch the faintest whiff of free publicity, they descend like a plague on a place like Ferguson. The biggest name in this business, the patron saint of the viral vampires, of course, is Al Sharpton.

He swept into the Ferguson fray early on, proclaiming at Michael Brown's funeral, "The policies of this country cannot go unchallenged."[113]

Months later, when the grand jury declined to indict Officer Wilson, Sharpton struck a harsher tone in attacking the justice system. As protests raged and West Florissant Avenue burned, Sharpton and professional Black Lives Matter protesters called the decision "an absolute blow to those of us that wanted to see a fair and open trial."[114] Never mind that the decision was made by a jury of Ferguson citizens who had reviewed all of the available evidence. Al Sharpton fomenting controversy and keeping his waning brand in the forefront is obviously more important. (The victor in the battle between the old hustlers like Sharpton and Jesse Jackson and the new Black Lives Matter leaders remains to be seen.)

Sharpton, for all his bluster (and he makes his living from bluster), is only part of a larger system that links mainstream political elites, largely from the Democratic Party, to the activists they use to get their base excited. It's a get-out-the-vote technique. In that way racial controversy is good for Democrats, because it feeds the mentality of victimhood they need to keep minority voters in America firmly in the *D* column. This is why progressives have pioneered the solutionless solution. Have you ever noticed how many hot-button issues for the Left have no real policy attached to them? America's great rights movements—the abolitionists, the suffragettes, the civil rights movement—each had a specific law they wanted passed. Those activists didn't care about which party, for instance, gave women the right to vote (it was Republicans, by the way). They had a goal. But what does #BlackLivesMatter want? Modern Democrats, by encouraging a hashtag over any particular reform, manage to keep "vote Democrat" the only action people can take. Why come up with solutions to incredibly hard problems like how to support local cops trying to clean up bad neighborhoods or the poor families who are scraping together a better life for their kids? It's much easier to come up with a slogan or hashtag and have everyone change their Facebook profile pic. Let loose the hashtags of war! (Not that I'll be excited when the Democrats are forced to name a policy that will remedy a real problem. Thanks to the law of bureaucratic replication, the solutions they propose always amount to nothing more than endless regulations, with expensive training and a bunch of federal paper pushers. None of it does anything except whet the endless appetite of government employee unions for more dues.)

Remember Vice President Joe Biden's comments during the 2012 campaign? At a stop in Danville, Virginia, a city where African Americans are the largest ethnic group, he told his audience that Mitt Romney and the Republicans were "gonna put y'all back in chains." The Pennsylvania native and current DC and Delaware resident even added a hint of a southern accent. They're not even especially subtle about it these days.

More recently, President Obama himself has come to the defense of the Black Lives Matter movement, which regularly protests against police officers. Obama said that the protests were based on "a legitimate issue that we've got to address" and that "we as a society, particularly given our history, have to take this seriously." The president went on to say that "the African-American community is not just making this up" and that the issues were "not just something being politicized," that "there's a history behind it and we have to take it seriously."[115]

For Obama, Biden, and the liberal elites of this country, along with their agitator foot soldiers in "movements" like Black Lives Matter, America has apparently not moved beyond the hate-fueled rancor of the Jim Crow era, and it never will. That's how the progressive narrative is preserved. Their play-book is very simple. If minorities are constantly scared into thinking that anyone besides the Democrats wants to put them "back in chains," and constantly reminded of the shameful history of injustices committed decades ago by people now long dead, the Democratic voter rolls will continue to swell. Let's not talk about the universality of the American dream or the American values of hard work and freedom of expression. There is no room for those old and creaky (and somehow, through the leftist lens, probably racist) notions. Focusing on identity politics is a much more efficient political strategy. It's the classic tactic of "divide and conquer"—divide the people and then conquer the ballot box.

The Left's lecturing is not directed at all Americans, not by a long shot. When President Obama says that "we as a society, particularly given our history" need to pay attention to Black Lives Matter protesters, he's not talking to his fellow liberals in the country's urban centers. He's talking to Flyover Nation. In the elite leftist view, the center of all of America's racial strife is the Flyover states, where every cop is secretly a Ku Klux Klan member and wakes up every morning with his sister-wife, chomping at the bit to go and *arrest'um sum black people!* I had an uncle who, before his death, was a cop in my home state of Missouri. Cops don't decide one day to ruin their lives and their family's lives by murdering an innocent simply because that innocent is black. While the president lectured Flyover Nation, the urban leftist enclaves, by contrast, are *pinkies out*, above reproach. Places like New York and San Francisco are supposed to be bastions of politically correct multicultural understanding, right?

Maybe not. After all, it was in New York City that some of the Black Lives Matter rhetoric was shown to have deadly real-world consequences.

On December 20, 2014, New York Police Department officers Rafael Ramos and Wenjian Liu were gunned down as they sat in their car in the Bedford-Stuyvesant section of Brooklyn. Their killer was twenty-eight-year-old Ismaaiyl Abdullah

Brinsley, who ran from the crime scene into a subway station and shot himself. Brinsley had arrived in New York on a bus that day, coming from Baltimore, where that morning he had shot and wounded his ex-girlfriend Shaneka Thompson. On his way to New York City, Brinsley had posted a photo of a handgun to his Instagram account with the following caption:

> *I'm putting wings on pigs today. They take 1 of ours . . . let's take 2 of theirs #ShootThePolice #RIPErivGarner #RIPMikeBrown. This may be my final post . . . I'm putting pigs in a blanket.*[116]

His hashtags referenced Michael Brown, killed in Ferguson the previous August, and Eric (whom Brinsley's typo referred to as "Eriv") Garner, a New York man killed during a struggle with NYPD officers that July. In Garner's case, as in Brown's, protests had erupted after a grand jury made the decision not to indict the police officer involved on criminal charges.

The protests that had been raging since that summer, whipped into a frenzy by professional activists, had given rise to sickening antipolice rhetoric. With no big election in the near term to pour that anger into, the energy had to be directed somewhere—and sustained as a get-out-the-vote effort for the next election. About a month before the killings of Ramos and Liu, protesters in New York had stumbled upon a course of action, chanting: "What do we want? Dead cops!" Police responding to a protest had also been attacked with trash cans, which *New York Post* columnist Bob McManus, writing the day after the murders, called "an escalation that culminated in yesterday's Bed-Stuy executions."[117]

Ismaaiyl Brinsley was a disturbed man with a criminal record and clear propensity for violence. But that in no way makes the motivation for his ultimate action any less clear: He wanted revenge. He wanted revenge because the rhetoric of a nation-wide protest movement told him that cops were the enemy, so he resolved to put "wings on pigs." His perverted sense of "justice" was clear: "They take 1 of ours . . . let's take 2 of theirs." It was a case of "us versus them." And "them" was anyone in a uniform with a badge.

The liberal spin brigade jumped into immediate action, of course. Unapologetic leftist New York mayor Bill de Blasio, who made no secret of his support for the Black Lives Matter protests in his city, called the killing "an assassination" as well as a "despicable act." He made those remarks in the hospital where the two officers were pronounced dead. During his visit, other NYPD officers turned their backs on him.

Al Sharpton took to Twitter to say he was "outraged" and reminded his followers that "we stress nonviolence as the only way to fight for justice." In a later interview Sharpton went further, stating: "This is not about trying to take things into our own hands. That does not solve the problem of police brutality."[118] Naturally, "Reverend" Al made sure to bring it back to "the problem of police brutality" before Officers Ramos and Liu were barely cold in their graves.

All of their platitudes couldn't hide the simple truth of the matter: The protesters who chanted their demand for "dead cops" and the leaders who supported them had—and still have—blood on their hands. It's the blood of Rafael Ramos, who left behind his wife, two sons, his friends and neighbors in his community of Glendale in Queens, and his fellow members of the congregation at Christ Tabernacle Church. It's the blood of Wenjian Liu, who came to the United States from China at the age of twelve and gave back to his adopted community by serving on the police force.

You'd think that would be a teachable moment for the professional agitators of Black Lives Matter and their backers in high places, like George Soros, who funded the Ferguson operation.[119] Alas, such logic finds no home among the professional Left ("Shocking!" said no one ever). Several months later, violent rhetoric was still a hallmark of Black Lives Matter's anti-police protests.

In St. Paul, Minnesota, some of their activists decided to launch a protest over the weekend of the 2015 Minnesota State Fair (because something as all-American as a state fair must somehow be inherently racist, right?). On August 29 they led a march down a highway near the fairgrounds, holding a large BLACK LIVES MATTER banner, along with other signs with messages like END WHITE SUPREMACY. The protesters were also provided with a police escort as they marched. As they made their way down the road—along with their taxpayer-furnished escort—they started up a tasteful chant: "Pigs in a blanket, fry 'em like bacon!"[120]

Calling police officers "pigs," especially when they're on the scene providing protection for your expression of your First Amendment rights, is so blatantly unoriginal that it kills brain cells without the benefit of alcohol. Has the activist crowd really not been able to come up with a more original insult since the anti–Vietnam War protest of the 1960s and '70s? But the next line—"fry 'em like bacon"—sounds more like a call to action. But what sort of action could it mean?

As it happened, a police officer had been killed just the previous evening in Houston, Texas. Around 8:30 p.m., Harris

County deputy sheriff Darren Goforth was filling up his squad car at a Chevron gas station when Shannon Miles came up behind him and shot him in the back of the head at point-blank range. When Deputy Goforth slumped to the ground, Miles continued shooting at him before fleeing the scene.

Does that sound like "frying 'em like bacon"?

When Harris County sheriff Ron Hickman held a press conference announcing Miles's arrest the next day, he explained that there was no known history or connection between him and the man he had murdered. The killing appeared to be completely unprovoked—unless you counted Deputy Goforth's profession as provocation. According to Sheriff Hickman, his officer "was a target because he wore a uniform."[121] It's worth remembering that Texas had seen a surge in Black Lives Matter activity earlier that summer, after a black woman named Sandra Bland was arrested following a traffic stop in Prairie View, some thirty miles from Houston, and subsequently hung herself in her jail cell.[122]

After the death of their comrade, Deputy Goforth, law enforcement officials in Harris County sounded a clear warning about the heated rhetoric that was continually being used to attack their profession. The district attorney, Devon Anderson, called Goforth's killing "an assault on the very fabric of our society" and a sign of "open warfare on law enforcement." She called on "the silent majority in this country to support law enforcement."[123] Sheriff Hickman delivered an accurate assessment of the threat of violent words turning into violent actions. "At any point when the rhetoric ramps up to the point where calculated, coldblooded assassinations of police officers happen, this rhetoric has gotten out of control," he said. Then he offered some blunt, no-bull Texas truth telling: "We've heard 'black lives matter.' All lives matter. Well, cops' lives matter, too. So why don't we just drop the qualifier and just say 'lives matter,' and take that to the bank."[124]

I live in Texas, and I know plenty of people in law enforcement. You can trust a seasoned Texas cop to get right to the point of something and not spend any time dancing around the issue. In the nasty debate over whose lives matter more, this was a much-needed dose of Flyover Nation wisdom.

Sheriff Hickman got it right. "Lives matter," period. No qualifiers needed. My life matters, my family's lives matter, my black friends and neighbors' lives matter, my Hispanic friends and neighbors' lives matter, and on and on. And because our lives matter, we all have the right to defend ourselves if we feel our lives are being threatened. Police officers, who put their lives on the line every day, have the right to defend themselves as well.

CHAPTER 7

Degrading Yourself and Calling It Equality

The second man to ever screw me over was William Jefferson Clinton. Of course, I didn't know it at the time. I was a frizzy-headed eighth grader who, the summer before the fall election, applauded enthusiastically as he played the saxophone on Arsenio Hall's show. He was everywhere I was: He was on MTV and VH1; he hung with the celebrities I followed; he visited late-night talk shows; he was pop culture. Democrats knew how to talk to the youth and that's why I liked them. They were the brand of youth, races, and women. At least, that's what I thought.

Flash forward to my freshman year of high school. Ever the Clinton supporter, I donned a Clinton/Gore pin on my backpack. I had Clinton/Gore stickers on my Trapper Keeper. I thought about how awesome their administration was while I slathered my face at night with Noxzema and blared Janet Jackson's "Rhythm Nation" on my purple ghetto blaster. And then *she* happened. Paula Jones. My girlfriends and I had already learned the art of cruelty in seventh grade, so we were certified mean girls by the time we were freshmen. We mocked her hair, her face, her determination to take down our president simply because she was forlorn. I had no idea about the rape accusations, the harassment accusations; all the media told me was that this fat white guy named Ken Starr was taking all of our money and spending it on graying President Clinton's hair. We discounted Juanita Broaddrick's story, dismissing it as the sordid tale of a jealous woman.

"All of these women are coming out of the woodwork because Clinton became president," we gossiped over the lunch table, repeating what we'd heard on TV. The Democrats had their lock on us because of what we thought they were, not for what they were in reality.

When Bill Clinton shook his nonaccusatory sausage knuckle at the cameras and intoned that he "Did. Not. Have. *Seckshul.* Relations. With. *That.* Woman," *that* woman being Monica Lewinsky, we all believed him.

"Of *course* there is a reason!" we enthusiastically conned ourselves.

"She's horrible," I told my mother while setting the table and listening to Tom Brokaw recite headlines in the background.

"Well, of course," my mother agreed. They had her too.

Feminists boisterously supported Clinton. Gloria Steinem, from behind her dinner plate–sized rose-colored hippie sunglasses, condemned the ravenous women who clawed at the president. Feminists supported him more than they supported his wife. That was the first thing that stood out to me. How must Hillary have felt?

Hillary held his hand during the interviews and stood beside him when he spoke, nodding her bob like a Dixiecrat hype man for Clinton's one-man act. I felt bad for her. Her story resonated with a thread from my childhood, a woman rendered *defeminate* by what began sounding like her husband's personal indiscretions.

Clinton's story unraveled, and all of us girls who had so wholeheartedly believed that he was the target of that "vast right-wing conspiracy" were politically stood up. The Clinton we knew wasn't there. The red-faced man who liked his Cokes with a lot of ice and waved at me in the parking lot of my school, the man who valued his wife and daughter and played sax on *Arsenio* was gone. In his place was a cautionary tale of putting faith in men, in politics, in anything but God.

When it was universally realized that Clinton was a philanderer, I accepted it and continued to support him—but something had changed. I recognized within myself that I had compromised an integral part of my beliefs in order to count myself as a supporter. It was a slow process, but politically it made me angry. I grew up knowing what marital infidelity was and the agony it causes families. That I had compromised my opposition to that for this president angered me. I was angry that Democrats had put us in this position. They knew the entire time; it was just a Victorian freak show centered around prolonging the inevitable. The women they trotted out at events and in interviews were tools, nothing more.

"What do you care?" barked a friend when I expressed doubt about our president over his infidelities. Feminists stopped accusing the women who came forward of lying; they stopped painting them as harlots and instead turned their fury on Ken Starr. They made the prosecutor the bad guy for Clinton lying under oath and then turned on the American public—who supported Democrats when they painted the women as harlots—when they didn't continue their enthusiastic support.

"He's married to his wife; he's not married to the country. Let them sort it out."

"Yes," I replied. *But if you can't honor an oath you made before God to your wife, how can you be expected to honor your oath to uphold the Constitution?* I thought. I didn't dare say it, lest I be treated the same as his accusers. That's when my path first parted from the Democrats and I began a long journey of recovery from the condition known as *Liberalus Feministus*.

When I was a college freshman I showed up to Grandma and Grandpa's once for Thanksgiving with my hair near shaved and my nose pierced. Grandma stared at me in horror. She didn't recognize me for the longest time and asked an aunt if Gale had picked up a lesbian hitchhiker while en route from St. Louis to the Ozarks. When she realized it was me, that I had cut off all my hair, that I had put a stud in my nose, her lips pursed and she wouldn't hug me or say hello. That was the first time I made Grandma mad. The second time was when I showed up for my first Christmas as a married woman and I pulled into Grandma and Grandpa's gravel drive with a Republican bumper sticker on my car. My uncle was in the inner circle of a well-known Democrat in Missouri who was running for senate. His opponent was a Republican named Jim Talent, whose sticker was on my bumper. As I exited the car and retrieved the side dish I had brought, my uncles, who held court in the drive, where they talked cars and hunting, drank beer, and smoked, raised an eyebrow at me. One uncle, a cigarette perched on his lip, drawled, "Girl, what's that sticker you got there on your car?"

"She got Talent's sticker on her car!" stage-whispered another.

"A Talent sticker?" stage-whispered a few to one another.

"Oh, man, wait until Uncle J sees this!" crowed a cousin.

By the time I had walked up the steps and into Grandma and Grandpa's tiny little house, word had gotten out that the grand-daughter who had shaved her hair "lesbian short" and pierced her face was now a *Republican*. It would have been more accept-able had I told the family that I was selling meth out of my gar-den shed in St. Louis County and stripping on the side in East St. Louis.

"Well!" said Grandma, passing through the crowd of kin gathered in her home. "I see you moved up to the city and done got *brainwarshed*!"

"I'm still the same, Grandma," I said, giving her a kiss.

I didn't get a spot at the adults' table for dinner, nor was I invited to play dominoes after dessert. My family secretly blamed my husband, but in reality he had nothing to do with it. It was because of my firstborn.

Before I was a conservative, I was a progressive feminist. I had my midlife crisis of sorts when I was twenty-one years old. When I discovered I was pregnant, I was in college, engaged, and not in any way financially stable. I was terrified. I knew almost nothing about babies. I assumed that I would have a daughter and could raise her to be the mirror image of me, a progressive feminist who would fight against systemic, patriar-chal oppression. Then the ultrasound technician told me I was going to have a son. *A boy.* I'd decided that I was going to have my son naturally, and I told my Grandma that I was going to skip the epidural. She crossed her eyes in exasperation and guilt-tripped me by telling me that she had delivered nine babies and she would have loved an epidural. Grandpa chimed in with exaggerated stories about how his mother had to gnaw on a strip of leather, hike up her skirt, and squat in the cornfield out back to bring him into the world.

"It's like you went to get educated and came back hating modern medicine," she said.

I was still pretty progressive at that point, diverging only on matters of abortion and the Second Amendment. I was still a third-wave feminist, and I was coming to terms with how to raise a *boy*. None of it made any sense until the moment the nurse placed my son in my arms moments after his birth. It was then that it *clicked*. In his face I found my future. I felt as if I were on a boat, pushing away from the dock of everything familiar, watching everything I was disappear into the fog as I set sail toward the unknown. This tiny boy now depended on me for everything, for life. I'd had a difficult birth and had been moments away from a cesarean when my OB determined that I would be able to pass his ginormous head. During one scary moment I wouldn't stop bleeding, orders were barked, my son's stomach was pumped, and my husband stood in the room, an expression of horror on his face. To his right his wife was bleeding out, possibly requiring surgery, and to his left his son had passed meconium in utero and was having his tiny stomach pumped.

"Go to Liam!" I said to him. It wasn't a decision. I would have died then and there for my son and would do so twenty times over for him. One night, while I was recovering in the hospital, hovering between consciousness and sleep, the nurses' station called me through my bed's monitor.

"Mrs. Loesch, your son is hungry. May we bring him in?"

My *son*.

Thoughts warp-sped into my mind as I nursed him, and I asked myself, *What have I done?* Up to this point I had spent my time making him, the male sex, the enemy. I had helped create a culture that was growing in hostility toward the male sex, a culture that ordained that substituting the matriarchy for the patriarchy was "equality." Through my prior activism I had helped construct a world prejudiced against him because he was born a boy. He had *privilege*, somehow. As a mother I was responsible for his upbringing, his emotional health, ensuring that he was a happy, well-adjusted child. Everything I had believed in was antithetical to my job now as his mother. Things that I had supported were harmful to his well-being. I recoiled from my former beliefs with visceral disdain. Gazing at my tiny boy I was born again, baptized by the fiery pain of birth, and part of this world with new purpose. Suddenly my long-held ideology and the reality of my circumstances collided: How could I continue railing against the travesties of the patriarchy, how could I continue my campaign against men, when here in my arms lay a boy, a boy whom his father and I were to raise into a man? How could I fill his head and heart with the poison I had been fed? How could I teach him as I had been taught, that men were oppressors, while I as a woman was cultivating my victimhood status as a very tool of oppression? When Liam was born, so was I—an intellectual rebirth, a spiritual rebirth, a rebirth of the heart. My instinct to protect this tiny person at all costs was overwhelming at times. Everything in my view sharpened into a clear perspective. The haze of ironic ideology was gone, and in its place was purpose. The change was remarkable and continued, a domino effect. Pillar after pillar, once erected to the false god of progressivism, toppled. Where previously I had been questionably prochoice with caveats, I became pro-life. I could not deny the life that I harbored, a separate identity from myself yet as dependent upon me as progressives are upon the state. I could not deny that teaching him to apologize for himself because he was a man was anything other than a form of abuse. I've always known the importance of a good father-daughter relationship, having felt the absence of one in my own life, but not until I had a son did I understand the supreme significance of the mother-son relationship. While today's mothers rage about protecting their daughters, shouting non sequiturs such as "Tell men not to rape!" I find fewer publicly vocal mothers protesting the war on their sons. There is a war over the heart and soul of the matriarchy and men are caught in between. There exists a real war on boys, on men, perpetuated by women, and only women can stop it.

I began noticing the war on boys after I had a son. I saw the glib "Boys suck, throw rocks at them" shirts. I saw the bias in popular culture as the fathers on sitcoms were portrayed as bumbling idiots. I was no longer part of the matriarchy and thus could see its effect. Men are ridiculed and demonized at every stage of life with barely any grace given to those early years because of their "male privilege." They're defamed in college. A number of stories surfaced within the past year detailing false accusations of rape made against male university students.

Columbia University student Emma Sulkowicz carried around a mattress as a whacked-out performance project after she accused fellow student Paul Nungesser of rape. Nungesser maintained his innocence and said that their two encounters had been consensual. Sulkowicz did not report the alleged attack initially and continued to send Nungesser texts and speak with him in the months after her alleged rape. Ashe Schow covered the story extensively in the *Washington Examiner*:

> *Facebook messages obtained by the Daily Beast contributor Cathy Young show that two days after Sulkowicz was allegedly beaten and choked, she responded to Nungesser's party invite by writing "lol yussss." She followed up that message by telling him: "Also I feel like we need to have some real time where we can talk about life and thingz" and "because we still haven't really had a paul-emma sesh since summmerrrrr."* [125]

A week later Sulkowicz invited Nungesser, whom she now refers to as her "rapist," to hang out. And a month after that, she responded to Nungesser's birthday message to her by saying: "I love you Paul. Where are you?!?!?!?!"

Six months later Sulkowicz would accuse Nungesser of previously raping her.

When police finally investigated, they found nothing. Both the police and Columbia cleared Nungesser, who continued to be harassed by Sulkowicz. Sulkowicz took to carrying her mattress around campus with her as a form of "protest." New York senator Kirsten Gillibrand referred to Nungesser as a "rapist" while speaking at a public event. Nungesser himself sued Columbia, claiming that the university condoned Sulkowicz's "gender-based discriminatory harassment."[126]

The lawsuit also notes that *Columbia Spectator* editor Teo Armus took photos of Nungesser at graduation—photos that were later published in other news outlets, "so that the world would recognize and remember the face of Emma's target." Armus has since, according to the lawsuit, "stalked" Nungesser, including seeking out his mother's employer in Germany.

Nungesser's lawsuit also includes a new section about the art show where Sulkowicz presented drawings of Nungesser over articles written about her mattress project. The lawsuit cites Columbia's policy regarding gender-based misconduct, including these examples: "Unwelcome remarks about the private parts of a person's body" and "Graffiti concerning the sexual activity of another person."

Sulkowicz's art project, which included drawings of Nungesser's genitals and depictions of the sexual act Sulkowicz claims occurred between them, would presumably fall under those categories. Yet Columbia did not prevent the images from being posted to be seen by the public, including Nungesser's parents, who were in town for the graduation.

In this case the boy was presumed guilty because the word of the girl was believed over his in the face of the facts. I wish I could say this was the only case, but this is becoming the rule, not the exception.

Rolling Stone published a farcical story by Sabrina Erdely that focused on gang-rape allegations made by a woman named "Jackie" against seven members of the University of Virginia's Phi Kappa Psi fraternity. Erdely never contacted the accused in the article and instead published the accusations as gospel truth. Jackie's story didn't add up: the dates, the fraternity, even the party at which the rape was said to have occurred. The Charlottesville police found no evidence to support Jackie's accusation, and friends of Jackie came forward to challenge her story. The man Jackie claimed had taken her to the party and encouraged the rape was discovered to be a fictitious, elaborate composite character that Jackie had likely made up (using a head shot of an old high school classmate, names from *Dawson's Creek*, and Internet phone numbers to fake texts to her friends) to make jealous another male student who had turned down Jackie's romantic advance. It all sounds very *Fatal Attraction*. By the time sleuths discovered it was an entirely made-up accusation and the Columbia School of Journalism shredded *Rolling Stone*'s credibility, the damage was done. The fraternity's reputation was in shambles, the university's dean was under fire, and the story had thrust campus rape into the national spotlight with exaggerated figures. The fraternity sued the magazine, the dean sued the magazine, *Rolling Stone*'s deputy managing editor gave his resignation, and the magazine that had once glorified the Boston bomber with a Jim Morrison–esque cover once again found itself the most reviled publication in America. All of this could have been avoided if Jackie hadn't falsely accused her fellow students of rape. If Erdely had actually performed the job of a journalist and chased the story instead of a narrative, this story would not have been published. The belief of *she* in a "he said/she said" created the environment for an irresponsible story such as this to germinate. Lives were ruined over this, a narrative based on gender discrimination—discrimination against men. Male college students are denied due process if accused of rape. The Affirmative Consent Project was born, with universities encouraging students who have sexual relations to photograph themselves with their signed mutual consent form.[127] California passed a state law requiring colleges that receive state funding to include such mutual consent agreements as part of their campus policy.

Universities began adopting policies that male students

were guilty until proven innocent, but in the cases of Nungesser, UVA, and "John Doe" who is suing Brown University over a false accusation, the truth didn't exonerate the accused. Schow notes that there are now over thirty men who are fighting back against various universities' lack of due process for those falsely accused of rape.

Feminists began sloganeering with "Teach men not to rape!"

Now here is the solutionless solution rising up again. How about "Teach women not to lie"? Why not teach women about *true* empowerment, an empowerment that comes by way of self-sustainment and hard work, not pretending that they're helpless victims in a sea of testosterone? Because that doesn't scare people into taking the only action they can: voting for the party with the catchiest social slogan.

Lying about rape not only makes it harder for *actual* rape victims to obtain justice but also produces a chilling effect that discourages real rape victims from speaking out: They're afraid that no one will believe them because some manipulative women cried wolf one too many times. Third-wave feminists believe that anyone who claims that she was raped deserves to be believed. Hillary Clinton tweeted: "Every survivor of sexual assault deserves to be heard, believed, and supported."

Whether or not that includes Kathleen Willey or Juanita Broaddrick was never made clear.

My husband's paternal grandmother once angrily remarked, after seeing a feminist protest on the nightly news: "These women just set back motherhood a hundred years." He had gone to visit her one evening and they were watching the nightly news together.

FLYOVER NATION

"These women have set us back a hundred years," said Grandma Loesch. "We fought hard to get out of the fields and these women put us right back in them," she said spitefully. Grandma Loesch was politically minded and outspoken. The matriarch of her family until she passed, Grandma Loesch raised ten children, all but three of them girls. She recognized her strength and relished her role in the home. While Grandpa Loesch traveled, obtained various college degrees, and built a real estate business, Grandma Loesch ran the roost. By the time I entered the picture and met her, she was nearly lost to Alzheimer's. I did get to *meet her* meet her once, though, when she had a rare moment of clarity the first time she met my first-born son, her great-grandson. She sat beside me on the sofa and stroked his fat hand.

"Oh, Dana," she said to me after my father-in-law, her son, told her about the baby, "he really is beautiful." She smiled at me before that spark in her eyes slipped away.

I have been most blessed in life to be surrounded by strong examples of female leadership. My own maternal grand-mother, Grandma Scaggs, was the matriarch of our family. She raised eight children while her husband, my grandfather, worked his fields and cattle. When I told her that I wanted to stay home for the first few years of my children's lives, she replied, "If you can do it, take advantage of it."

I think it vulgar that modern-day, third-wave feminism is so quick to downplay the natural talents and strengths of women. It is a movement that has outlived its usefulness and is so disfigured it doesn't even qualify as a hopeless caricature of what it was in the days of (pro-lifer) Susan B. Anthony. During Anthony's day feminists marched, supported by Republicans, for the recognition of their right to vote. Today feminists march, supported by Democrats, for free birth control pills. When Sandra Fluke, fresh from backpacking across Europe and drinking wine with her boyfriend, held a press conference on Capitol Hill and pretended it was a hearing, she lamented her lot in life, that as a student at a pricey university she couldn't control her libido and thus was paying thousands of dollars a year for birth control pills specifically for her sexual recreation. (She tried to parlay her fifteen minutes into a political career and failed spectacularly, likely because her constant panhandling wore on people.) The math didn't add up, and many women across the country asked why Fluke's birth control was so expensive when theirs cost just a few bucks at Target or Costco.

Progressives shouted and screamed for conservatives to get out of their bedrooms, and with this issue they added a delicious ironic caveat: Stay out of their bedrooms except to pay for what goes on *in* the bedroom. You can't have it both ways. If I'm to be forced to invest in someone's sexual recreation, I should at least get to publicly question her morality when her libido warrants a several-thousand-dollar-a-year birth control bill.

The choice for women is *before* conception. I've never opposed birth control. In fact, the GOP doesn't either, which is why it's pushed for some time to render birth control available over the counter. The Left is against it, particularly Cecile Richards, head of Planned Parenthood, as it would eliminate the bait to visit her abortion mill. Heaven forbid we give pro-choice women choices. The shrieking from the Left, led by the Skeksis of the House, Nancy Pelosi, accused Republicans of blocking women's access to birth control. They painted a picture of chubby, white congressmen throwing themselves in front of women as though they were blocking a goal every time a woman attempted to enter a pharmacy and purchase birth control. Since insurance covers birth control for health reasons such as endometriosis (I know, as I suffered from a mild yet painful form and it was offered as an option by my OB/GYN and covered by my insurance), perhaps, Republicans suggested, women who seek birth control for sexual recreation could pay for it themselves. Democrats were outraged, feminists were outraged, and they all took to the airwaves to collectively make that sound that the Wicked Witch of the West made when Dorothy doused her with water. It's a quasi reverse pimping: Americans forced to toil and pay for a woman's *sex-ay par-tay fun times*!

Some members of my Flyover family were appalled. No one, man or woman, should hold a press conference and ask the nation to pay for their birth control.

"Well, heck, I didn't ask no one to pay for my condoms," said a cousin in a very too-much-information moment. Other members of my family revered Sandra Fluke as some sort of folk hero. A begging-for-birth-control folk hero.

Another disconnect I had with feminism came when I realized that the third wave was encouraging women to value themselves not according to their own strengths as members of the female sex but rather by how well they measured up against men. Borrowing patriarchal systems of measurement for everything from pay to combat seems oxymoronic. Doing so inherently shows that they themselves view our female sex as the weaker of the two. The Pentagon recently declared that combat roles will open up to women. For years activists who have never eaten an MRE in the desert heat or left family for months at a time to serve their country wanted to dictate over military commanders how the branches should be ordered. We are to pretend that women have the same bone density and muscle mass as men so as not to hurt feelings with political incorrectness. The Marines were under enormous pressure to lower their standards for entry so as to accommodate women who failed physical tests, even after it was shown that women fared worse in combat-skills tests and suffered double the number of injuries.[128] General Martin Dempsey once said:[129]

> *If we do decide that a particular standard is so high that a woman couldn't make it, the burden is now on the service to come back and explain to the secretary, why is it that high? Does it really have to be that high?*

We're talking about reducing the effectiveness of our military to satisfy political correctness. Most women are not suited for combat, with very, very few exceptions, the Kurdish Women's Protection Units being one. I have the privilege of knowing another such exception, a member of my family, a woman who set a record for sit-ups in the army. But we should settle for being surprised by the exceptions, not changing the rules.

The irony is that you never hear anyone saying all women should have to register for the draft. In the battle over "inequality," an illogical premise lingers: So long as boys are forced to register with the Selective Service upon their eighteenth birthday, the same requirement should befall girls. If combat roles are to be open to all women, then so too should the draft. Until that time, forcing boys but not girls to register for the draft is gender discrimination. If I have to sign up my sons, you feminists better get prepared to sign up your daughters.

There are not a lot of business opportunities in the town where my family resides. You either work at the quarry or the bank, teach at the small school, find a factory in the region, or work at the Rest'urnt. Every one of my aunts and a few of my cousins worked at the Rest'urnt as waitresses. When we cousins were little, we would tear around the whole town and take our parents' loose change inside and buy Cokes with lots of ice. There was no shame in being a mother who stayed home and there was no shame in getting work outside of the home, either. Parenting, mothering, fathering is about making ends meet, period. Working for your children so they have food to eat is the same job as preparing that food *for* them to eat. Staying at home to raise your children and working to make sure they have what they need to live are *both* ways to mother. There is more judgment about women's roles outside of Flyover Nation than inside of it. Every insecurity possessed by the coasts is projected onto Flyover and the people happily and voluntarily contained therein. People in Flyover are proud to be stay-at-home moms, homemakers, and homebodies. Women are proud to act like ladies and men like gentlemen.

We live in a world where feminists define female empowerment by how well they can measure up to male expectations. They conflate femininity and feminism and view as limitations and burdens the natural strengths and weaknesses of the female sex. Third-wave feminists tossed out the yardstick by which these things are measured and instead insist that society measure women by the same yardstick as it measures men. (A brief history lesson: First-wave feminism a hundred years ago wanted the right to change the laws. Second-wave feminism a half century ago wanted to change the culture. Third-wave feminists now want to change reality.) Third-wave feminism presupposes that the previous distinction of measure is sexist. It claims to want equal pay in the workplace yet demands this while generally taking more time away from work for maternity leave and child care. Third-wave feminists want to retain qualities unique to the female sex yet demand equal treatment to men while doing so. If the practice of fairness is the focus, this is wholly unfair.

When faced with this dichotomy, the third wave blames masculinity.

For the past few years women have been lectured on the subject of "pay inequality."

No, women do not make less money than men for the same job anymore.[130] Feminists demanded choices, got choices, and subsequently whined about the result of the choices they made using their own free will. If there is a pay discrepancy, it is because of *choices.* The *Wall Street Journal* sums it up thus:

> *The Bureau of Labor Statistics (BLS) notes that its analysis of wages by gender does "not control for many factors that can be significant in explaining earnings differences."*
>
> *What factors? Start with hours worked. Full-time employment is technically defined as more than 35 hours. This raises an obvious problem: A simple side-by-side comparison of all men and all women includes people who work 35 hours a week, and others who work 45. Men are significantly more likely than women to work longer hours, according to the BLS. And if we compare only people who work 40 hours a week, BLS data show*

that women then earn on average 90 cents for every dol-
lar earned by men.

Career choice is another factor. Research in 2013 by
Anthony Carnevale, a Georgetown University econo-
mist, shows that women flock to college majors that
lead to lower-paying careers. Of the 10 lowest-paying
majors—such as "drama and theater arts" and "coun-
seling psychology"—only one, "theology and religious
vocations," is majority male.

Conversely, of the 10 highest-paying majors—including
"mathematics and computer science" and "petroleum
engineering"—only one, "pharmacy sciences and admin-
istration," is majority female. Eight of the remaining nine
are more than 70% male.

Other factors that account for earnings differences
include marriage and children, both of which cause
many women to leave the workforce for years. June
O'Neill, former director of the Congressional Budget
Office, concluded in a 2005 study that "there is no gen-
der gap in wages among men and women with similar
family roles." [131]

It's men, not women, who put in longer hours at work.[132]
The wage gap is a myth. There *is* a gap, to be sure, and according to *Forbes*, it's that of women in their twenties outearning
men.[133] Women are now *more* likely to have college degrees
than men are.[134] According to the last census, *Time* reports,
"young women are driving the change. In the 25–34 age group,
37.5% of women have a bachelor's degree or higher, while
only 29.5% of men do." So when men are penniless and uned-
ucated, will feminists *then* finally claim equality?

Today's feminists equate sleaze with empowerment. They call it "brave," and "empowered." Degrading oneself just to show that you've the freedom to do it is "empowering" or something. Modesty is ridiculed. Being a lady is ridiculed. Today's woman is "brave" if she man-spreads on a stool with her Michelin Man rolls spilling over the top of her underpants (Amy Schumer for Annie Leibovitz). She's brave if she disrobes in every episode as a plot device (Lena Dunham). When women aren't conflating skankiness with empowerment, they're pretending victimhood is empowerment's equal.

Strength is a sin and weakness is a virtue. It's a reason why the third wave hates masculinity.

David French in *National Review* wrote of a culture shift, one among honor, dignity, and victimhood:

> As western civilization built an elaborate rule of law, "dignity culture" replaced honor culture. In a dignity culture, in Haidt's words, people "foreswear violence, turn to courts or administrative bodies to respond to major transgressions, and for minor transgressions they either ignore them or attempt to resolve them by social means." The southern culture of my childhood was a hybrid, where honor was earned. Violence was certainly possible in this culture, but all parties would appeal to authority when life or limb hung in the balance. The bottom line was that you either ignored minor transgressions or you learned to step up, personally, to deal with offense. The honor and dignity cultures, however, face new competition from an insidious development:

victim culture. In victim culture, people are encouraged "to respond to even the slightest unintentional offense, as in an honor culture. But they must not obtain redress on their own; they must appeal for help to powerful others or administrative bodies, to whom they must make the case that they have been victimized." This is the culture of the micro-aggression, where people literally seek out opportunities to be offended. Once "victimized," a person gains power—but not through any personal risk. Indeed, it is the victim's hypersensitivity and fragility that makes them politically and socially strong. In victim culture, a person cultivates their sense of weakness and fragility, actively retarding the process of growing up.

Not only is this mindset destabilizing—there is high incentive for conflict, with little to no personal risk to balance the desire for vengeance—it's unmanly. In victim culture, a person cultivates their sense of weakness and fragility, actively retarding the process of growing up. There is zero incentive to mature, because maturity can actually decrease your power and influence. [135]

This victim culture is killing American masculinity—which is bizarre, because as you'll see later in my chapter on culture, pop culture *craves* it. Third-wave feminism is so preoccupied with obliterating American manhood that it's ignoring the real patriarchal attack on women: the transgender movement.

Last summer Bruce Jenner, the guy to whom my older cousins looked up and bought Wheaties because of, the guy who was the greatest athlete on the planet, announced that he was going to start living his life pretending that he's a woman. When I was younger, men who dressed up as women were called drag queens or, as per Dr. Frank-N-Furter, "sweet transvestites." Apparently those words are now stricken from the English language by the PC police, as people pretending to be the opposite sex are now referred to as "transgendered."

Jenner's "coming out" as a chosen female identity was done with Diane Sawyer in a much-hyped prime-time interview, a perfectly timed promotional vehicle for Jenner's spin-off reality show, *I Am Cait*. The show followed Jenner's "transition" from pretending to be a female privately to pretending to be one publicly, all the time. Jenner showed off his new closet to Sawyer and his new collection of large-size day heels. He grew out his hair and sported shiny blowouts. He discussed how he was learning to apply makeup and how women have it so much harder than he fathomed because we wear makeup nearly daily. He got breast implants and was named *Glamour*'s "Woman of the Year." Jenner posited himself as the face of the transgender *movement*. Progressives in LA and NYC feted Jenner, called him "brave," bestowed upon him the Arthur Ashe Courage Award at the ESPYs. Jenner showed women that men could be better women than they, provided they had Jenner's cash to splurge on jaw shaving, silicone, and other cosmetic surgeries. Being a woman, said *Glamour* with its choice, is a commodity. The female sex can be bought.

The craziest thing here is not that he is now a she but that the viral vampires—who never seemed to care about this before—suddenly decided that anyone not publicly bursting with praise for Jenner was a bigot.

Elsewhere this saga played out in gyms and schools across the

United States. A Planet Fitness (a fake gym that lacks a real squat rack and apparently frowns upon actual muscle gains) revoked the membership of a woman who, after finishing her workout, walked into the women's locker room to find a tall man changing. Concerned, Yvette Cormier reported it to the front desk staff, who condemned her for her "inappropriate" remark and stated that the gym has a "no judgment policy," meaning that if men want to identify as women for the day and change in the ladies' locker room, they are allowed. Apparently Planet Fitness failed to inform Cormier (or other members) of this when signing her contract and taking her money for gym membership.

My cousins' school, Hillsboro High School in the same-named district in Hillsboro, Missouri, saw female and male students walk out because a male high school senior who calls himself "Lila" Perry demanded use of the girls' locker rooms and restrooms—despite having been offered a faculty restroom. The senior said he was transgendered and the previous year had begun wearing makeup and girls' clothing to school. The students staged a walkout in response. I spoke with one of the high school females on my television program. In a nervous voice she explained that it is hard enough to be a young woman going through puberty without the added weight of changing in front of a boy in the locker room. The female students protested the invasion of their privacy and modesty; the tall young man at the center of the controversy accused the girls of being bigots for not wanting to change or use the restroom along with him. Perry, a big senior male student, verbally attacked the female students for not acquiescing to his demands. The girls at the school, raised to protect their bodies and their modesty, now found themselves being shamed for doing so by this young man.

Men pretending to be women are not women. Women pretending to be men are not men. As a woman, I'm more offended by the former. It's the height of sexism to assume that the entirety of a woman is summed up by a pair of fake boobs, a blowout, makeup, and high heels. It's sexist for any man to think he can do any of this and tuck or cut and—voilà!—instant woman. Being a woman is so much more than that, yet this new breed of patriarchy lectures to women that all we are is *cosmetic*, all we are is silicone, filler, MAC, and Louboutin. That's what it is—an attack by the patriarchy. I was once lectured on Twitter by a man pretending to be a woman that I couldn't *possibly* understand what it is to struggle as a woman. No? Growing up with my single mother? Living through the embarrassing milestone of my first period? Growing up flat-chested until my sophomore year of high school, when everything changed and I was oblivious to it and the reactions that came with it? Struggling with society's expectations of female beauty in a society that wants to sexualize girls before they are old enough to drive? Being looked down upon by some boys for not "putting out"? Getting married and realizing that I had to share a bathroom with a boy for the rest of my life? Having my first child and feeling insecure about my mothering skills, my dinner-making skills, my skills as a provider? Feeling the guilt that only mothers can know over working away from home and lying awake at night wondering if I'm doing the right thing or if he would be better off with me home? Worrying about him as he discovers girls and dealing with the first girl to break his heart? I love dads. They are partners with us moms. But just as I will never fully understand the problems with which dads struggle, so dads will not fully comprehend the problems with which mothers struggle—nor will any man, for that matter. These people need mental and emotional help, not enablers who assist them into a false reality. If your friend tries to do something to harm himself, to cut off his arm with a power tool, you stop him. You don't encourage his fantasy of being "trans-abled."[136]

What's even worse, a new crop of parents are now treating this as a "condition." Parents whose children are too young to drive a car (or, in some cases, even wipe their backsides) are allowed to determine if they want to stuff their tiny bodies with dangerous hormone treatments, stall puberty, and in some cases surgically remove their copulatory organs. It's child abuse. When I was a little kid I wanted to grow up and be a flower, but my mother, rather than indulge my trans-kingdomness, instead shattered my dreams and informed me that I was a human girl and would grow up to be a human woman. Children need boundaries. They need parents, advocates, not enablers.

Brave. In our current culture true *bravery* is modesty, which progressives conflate with shame. Bravery is acting like a man when you're a man, though as we're about to see, some of us are forgetting what being a man even means.

CHAPTER 8

Forgetting Who We Are

The problem isn't just for women, whom progressivism has reduced to birth control panhandlers who protest with feces and feminine-hygiene products. Through feminism, men are being shamed for their masculinity. Society is trying desperately to eliminate it from the male sex altogether, while something curiously opposite is happening in pop culture.

Everyone swoons over Daryl Dixon on *The Walking Dead*, but where I come from there exist a million Daryl Dixons: greasy, dirty denim–wearing, bow-hunting, coon-skinning country boys—boys who could take care of them and theirs if the world as we know it ended in one fiery flash, leaving nothing behind but dead branches and ash. To echo Mugatu from *Zoolander*, hillbilly is so hot right now. Hillbilly is *couture*. Hillbilly comes to mind when you think of people doing things for themselves.

The characters that all the girls want to be with and all the boys want to be like are Rick Grimes and Daryl Dixon, particularly Dixon. Dixon is a bowman. In season four of the series Dixon runs up on a group of thugs while looking for Beth. An altercation ensues and Dixon aims his crossbow at the leader of the pack.

"A bowman. I respect that," the man says. "A man with a rifle, you could have been some kind of photographer or soccer coach back in the day, but a bowman's a bowman through and through." When women are given the choice between a skinny metrosexual who says words like "product" when describing hair gel, has his jeans tailored, and needs a mechanic to change his windshield wipers and an outdoorsman who can live off the land, protect his family, and service his own car with his own rough hands, the latter will win every single time. Gleaming, sweaty, strong masculinity is unmatched in the dating world. It's a necessary counterweight to femininity. It's also under attack. Daryl is a favorite because Daryl is the first person you'd pick for your dodgeball team. Daryl is who you'd choose for company if you were ever stranded on an island. He's the guy you'd want to have by your side in a foxhole. Daryl is masculinity, vulnerability, sustainability, pure *ability* wrapped up in a leather jacket with angels' wings embroidered on the back. Daryl is pure Flyover Nation. Daryl lives in the real world, not some societal construct of people who've for so long been inside concrete jungles that they've forgotten how the middle of the nation lives. The Daryls of the world don't wear leathers for fashion; they wear them so as not to get road rash if they fall off their bikes. They wear flannels because they're warm, they're versatile, and the pattern hides grease stains well. When I was a kid I remember wondering how in the world my grandpa ever got clothes. The man had never set foot inside a mall, a Target, or a Walmart in his life. He wore Wranglers, work boots for the field, a brown belt, an undershirt, and a plaid (short-sleeved, spring and summer) or flannel (fall and winter) shirt with a hat every single day of his life. A pack of Marlboro Reds stuck out of his back left jeans pocket and a pair of work gloves stuck out of the right. He wore an old brown fedora for fancy occasions. The only known colors on Grandpa's color wheel were white, black, and brown. Every item on his person served a purpose.

I once saw a guy in Manhattan dressed like my grandpa. I was in NYC for Fox and had ducked into a Yelped café not far from Radio City Music Hall for coffee and a snack after my radio program and before taping *Red Eye*. I stood behind him in line. He wore clean, unsecured work boots that squeaked when he stepped, Wranglers, a flannel, and a sock hat. A pair of leather driving gloves protruded from his back jeans pocket with the fingers artfully splayed. His sleeves were rolled back enough to reveal his bracelets and he had the beginnings of a beard. He wore a sock hat even though it was nearly eighty degrees. His clothes were perfectly tailored and ironed. A perfectly conditioned brown leather messenger bag hung low across his frame. For a moment I wondered if there was a small farm tucked away in the city somewhere, perhaps a logging area nearby. I had grabbed the last green juice to drink in makeup after my coffee. He suddenly changed his mind at the register, went back to the upright cooler, and realized that that final serving of green juice he had seen was in my hand. He glared at me for a second before sighing a dramatic Bette Midler–quality sigh, returning to the register, and saying in a strained, overenunciated fashion, "Never. Mind. I guess I'm *not* going to get juice now after all."

That's when I realized that he was a hipster.

Not just any hipster, mind you—the genus of New York hipster has evolved into several different species, different subsets.

Where originally you had the hipster who listened only to vinyl, now you have a dozen or so varieties, each as annoying as the others. What I witnessed that afternoon at that NYC café is the most recent classification of hipster, known as the lumbersexual. The lumbersexual is the type of hipster who wants to look as though he just walked out of the forest fresh from a day of chopping wood to heat his log cabin that night. Lumbersexuals wear exclusively Columbia, North Face, and L.L.Bean. The image speaks to an unspoken acknowledgment and visceral craving.

The *New York Times*, a publication I don't read if I can avoid it, published an op-ed by what I can only imagine is a skinny lumbersexual who carries a "murse." It was called "27 Ways to Be a Modern Man," and after I read it my ovaries needed emotional therapy.

Number 16:

The modern man lies on the side of the bed closer to the door. If an intruder gets in, he will try to fight him off, so that his wife has a chance to get away.

Because he's a giant pansy and doesn't own a gun?
Number 25:

The modern man has no use for a gun. He doesn't own one, and he never will. [137]

Oh, wow, I had no idea I was so prescient. Going back to number 16, can the "modern man" even throw a punch? This is what passes as modern masculinity on the coasts. Sometimes I think these guys are the true transgendered. The editorial should really bear the title "27 Ways to Be a Beta Man."

Progressives have a longing for authenticity, for a deeper meaning to fill a hole in themselves that no number of wheatgrass smoothies can fill. You can see it in the holiday hillbillies making their occasional trips into the heartland to recapture something they lost. You can see it in the lumbersexuals, who think they can dress the part of a real man without having to make the sacrifices a real man finds himself making. You can see it in the Oprah-fication of the word "spiritual," as the coastals try to get enlightened without the Light and try to build a Kingdom of Heaven with no King.

They don't want to admit that there is a place they can find all the things they're longing for, and it's not a hot yoga studio.

When I was younger I'd attend morning service with my grandmother and aunts while my mother worked back in the city. Everyone was in a floral dress, some of the ladies wore hats, and panty hose were a requirement even in August and even with open-toed shoes. We'd all file in, and the satisfaction in Brother Jim's eyes would grow as the pews filled. He'd launch into one of his fire-and-brimstone sermons, occasionally wiping the sweat from his brow with a folded white handkerchief he kept in his breast pocket. My cousins and I would cast a side-eye glance at one another to see who was paying attention. Grandma had one of those little accordion fans she'd use and would often say "amen" more for the benefit of others than for herself. Sometimes she would rest her voice on the *n* in "amennnnn" as a verbal underscore. My cousins and I learned how to pretend to be enthralled by the sermons even if we had no idea what was being preached. Afterward everyone would make the weekly Sunday postchurch pilgrimage to Grandma and Grandpa's house, where she would hold court in the kitchen and the aunts would form a ring around the small dining room table with coffee, cigarettes, and gossip. It was their own sort of "church." The stories these women shared at the table were far more interesting to me than what I'd heard from Brother Jim (no offense, I was a kid!).

"Did you hear so-and-so ran off with so-and-so's husband the other day at the tavern?" one aunt would ask in a shocked tone.

"Noooo!" the other aunts would murmur.

"Oh, yes, she did," the aunt would continue, tapping her cigarette on the edge of the ashtray at the center of the table. I think she did it for dramatic effect. "She done run off with him and told so-and-so that she was leavin' with so-and-so."

"Harlot," Grandma would mutter. During church I learned about what sin does to the body and soul; from the stories around Grandma's dining room table I learned how it wrecks families and marriages. Plus, the gossip was better than an episode of one of Grandma's soap opera "stories." (Her favorite was *The Bold and the Beautiful*. I mocked that name so much. As in "Not only are they bold, but also, they are beautiful." It always began with people angrily yet slowly turning around and stating intently at the camera.) Sitting around my grandma's dining room table was like sitting around a campfire telling stories. I sometimes wondered, at least as a kid, where I learned the most about God: at Grandma's, hearing all the ways that the townsfolk violated His laws, or from Brother Jim's sermons. People learn more through stories and entertainment, the domain of culture, than from basic lectures. It's why movies, music, television, and art are all so successful as vessels for messaging. Flyover isn't often represented in the best way. For a long time Hollywood only ever wanted to portray Flyover as a suffocating, small-town setting from which the protagonist is desperate to escape. Flyover folks were slow-talking, one-toothed hillbillies who gummed their corn on the cob and only ever shopped at Walmart—which, by the way, whatever is wrong with Walmart?

Oh, I know, there's the big battle between union bosses and the Waltons over unionizing the place; I'm talking beyond that. Walmart has gotten a bad reputation with people who would prefer to pay more for the same item at a more "upscale" retailer. I love Walmart, particularly Super Walmarts. When my boys were teeny tiny it was the only place I could go and shop without someone having a meltdown. The one in my area had a McDonald's inside, and I relished feeding my children salty, GMO-loaded nuggets and fries to keep them happy while I perused the aisles with my meticulously edited grocery list. Super Walmart is the only place you can go to get your car's tires balanced, get your eyes checked, do some banking, get a family portrait at Olan Mills in front of a fall vignette, and purchase a gun and ammo, a six-foot-tall lawn Santa, a box of tampons, and a pound of hamburger meat *all at once*. God bless America. I could also do all of this while wearing my Paul Frank monkey pajama pants, if I so chose, because it's America and *I do what I want*. The moms who have all the time in the world to apply photo shoot–ready makeup and make every second of their lives Instagrammable have full-time nannies, fake raising children, or are sleepless beings.

Whenever society targets and attempts to demonize Flyover Nation by making it the subject of ridicule in entertainment, we know we're on the right track. Unfortunately for society, I think they've epically failed these past several years. For instance, Ron Swanson was my favorite character on *Parks and Recreation* before that sitcom ended, and it was my favorite sitcom *because* of Swanson. I don't watch a lot of television but always made a point to DVR *Parks and Recreation*. Swanson was straight no chaser, hysterically concise, and all the best parts of Flyover. I don't want to prejudge the show's writers—though I feel almost compelled to, since statistically Flyover is so often mocked in entertainment—but I can't imagine coastal Hollywood writers purposefully making a Flyover town so eccentrically lovable and the conservative character on the show the first you'd pick for your fantasy dodgeball team.

Christianity changed culture; it changed the world. It ushered in an understanding of grace and forgiveness. Jesus is the most magnificent storyteller and God's Word is the best-selling book of all time, yet the industry of telling stories is dominated by those who oppose His teachings, His influence, and the work of His disciples. The response of most of Christendom has been to segregate ourselves away from the secular world and create an entirely separate sphere of art, music, film, publishing, and education. Instead of using our talents to infiltrate and serve an unsuspecting world, we've partitioned ourselves off to make music for the choir. I don't say this to be cruel but rather to highlight how I once was lost. One of the verses that had the most impact on my viewpoint was Jesus's instruction in Matthew 10:16: "I am sending you out like sheep among wolves. Therefore be as shrewd as snakes and as innocent as doves."

I noticed at some point in my youth that Christians stopped going out in popular culture. I'm not talking about missionary work in other countries; I'm not talking about serving on the streets of America; I'm talking about creating art, creating music, weaving together stories, and producing films, all of which arguably serve as the greatest tools of witness the modern age has ever beheld. When Christians did return to the battlefield, it was to take their tools and segregate themselves in the *Christian* music industry, in the *Christian* film industry, in the *Christian* publishing industry, in *Christian* education. Why? Because some viewed the fight as unwinnable. (What was the movie you saw with a man of the cloth in it who wasn't the villain? *The Exorcist*? If they remade that movie now, they'd find a way to make it about demons' rights.)

Some believed that you could fight the good fight not on the battlefield where the conflict is actually taking place but in the safety of your backyard. I say none of this to be cruel but rather to instruct on how I was lost. As a Flyover girl growing up and branching out of the Midwest, I found my influences growing more and more secular until there was no light left. If I wanted a positive message I had to seek it, and society makes even the simple act of *seeking* shameful. It's amazing: A society that speaks out against "slut shaming" has no problem with "values shaming." I knew there existed Christian bookstores, but as an older teen I felt so far removed from what I had known as a child that I couldn't bring myself to walk through the doors of such a place. I feared instant judgment, an absence of grace, and it was clearly established as an entirely separate world. Christian artists didn't even chart on *Billboard*. There were scant few who ever made it to the mainstream; they weren't represented in the fashion magazines; they just disappeared from the prevalent culture. Think of this: Christianity, completely unrepresented in modern mainstream culture. It's not about trying to be "of the world" but about fighting for those lambs in it.

I was grateful for the advent of iTunes and the explosion of social media. There exists evil on social media, just as there is evil in the world, and all manner of inappropriateness, but social media has also closed the gap between what were once the mainstream and Christian cultures. Case in point: I had never listened to explicitly "Christian" music. I knew none of the Christian artists, none of their songs, nothing about their industry. The way iTunes categorizes its music, the Christian genre receives representation on the home page of the app. Through that I saw a song from Casting Crowns called "Praise You in This Storm." I previewed it and loved it so much I purchased it. Through that band I discovered more Christian artists, newly arranged praise and worship music, and more. Imagine how many others like me were able to explore and expand their faith through the vein of music because of an app. The explosion of social media sparked a revival in Christian culture. Long-form blogging is officially dead, having been killed off by the next evolution on social media, microblogging sites like Twitter, Instagram, Pinterest, Tumblr, and so on, yet it helped launch a movement born of faith and showcasing simple, faithful living. The previous generation of Christians may have forsaken culture, arts, and entertainment to, as they believed, protect their families from an increasingly aggressive secularism, but the subsequent generation has not only embraced the culture of social media but is using it to evangelize, to connect, to organize. Christians, in fact, have been so aggressive with their use of social media that they are holding their own in the medium against the secular world.

I really don't think that this would have been possible, or as possible, had it not been for *The Passion of the Christ*. Critics were doubtful Mel Gibson could pull it off, especially after learning that he had upped the ante and subtitled the film, which was in entirely in Aramaic. Gibson's film was a possibly unintended Rorschach test: *Slate*'s David Edelstein said of it:

> *You're thinking there must be something to* The Passion of the Christ *besides watching a man tortured to death, right? Actually, no: This is a two-hour-and-six-minute snuff movie—The Jesus Chainsaw Massacre—that thinks it's an act of faith.* [138]

The critical Left, which champions infanticide, found Jesus's death *too violent.* They focused on the violence rather than on the awe-inspiring fact that despite what we (all of us— if you've sinned, one of those lashes on Christ's back is from you) did to Christ, He begged Father God from the cross to forgive us, for "they know not what they do," and still (!) died for our sins. I will live all my life and hope only to come close to understanding a love as magnanimous as this.

The biblical epic opened on February 25, 2004, and is the highest-grossing R-rated (for violence) film in American history. Its opening-weekend earnings made it the fourth-highest earner in 2004. Mel Gibson, the troubled but brilliant director, famously eschewed traditional marketing to rely solely on Christian support. He did some smaller television ad buys but mainly relied on church groups and Christian organizations. Not since Cecil B. DeMille's *The Ten Commandments* had there been such a picture on the silver screen. This shook Hollywood to its core. People there couldn't believe a Christian film—a subtitled Christian film, no less—could be a blockbuster. It was the appetite of Christendom that propelled it, and the Weinsteins of the film world took notice. Because of the success of this film more Christian films have been, and are being, made. Television saw what happened in film and began its quest to replicate the success.

As I mentioned earlier, the Robertson family is one such example.

Fifteen years ago, heck, ten years ago, no one would have imagined that a humble, faithful family from Flyover America would become one of the most powerful and successful entities in television. The focus of their program is always their faith, highlighted in their family and business practices. Their story is one that is uniquely American: a comeback story. America loves a comeback story and Christians love a redemption story. They are one and the same with the Robertsons. Patriarch Phil Robertson did his wife and sons wrong, repented, and transformed from a humble duck caller in a Louisiana shack to part of a family empire. Flyover Nation saw in the Robertsons what they see in their own families each and every day. The Robertsons never hid from their past mistakes; they humbly submitted themselves to God and allowed themselves to be used as a powerful example of God's love and mercy. They didn't act proud; they remained the same humble, bandanna-bedecked Louisiana folks they were before the show exploded on A&E. Faith is about grace and redemption. Flyover Nation understands this. Some people who watched the Robertsons had previously believed themselves not good enough to walk the path of a Christian. They then heard about Phil's story, or the struggles of the other family members, and realized it's about admitting you need help, admitting that you aren't perfect and that you need God. The Robertsons showed that faith isn't about excusing sin but that grace and justice exist, along with forgiveness. This message played out on prime-time television one night a week, and Phil won the war over ending each episode in prayer.

I attended the first Duck Commander NASCAR race in Texas a couple of years back and spent some time talking with the family for my show on the *Blaze*. Every person attending was not just a NASCAR fan but also a Robertson fan. One of our producers, a born and bred California boy, was startled at the number of long-haired, camo-clad attendees. It looked like one of my family reunions. Hank Williams Jr. blasted over loudspeakers and men smoked meat in huge portable pits; the only thing missing was a game of washers and a couple of my blue-haired, pursed-mouth great-aunts passing silent judgment on everyone drinking beer. There is a simple, unpretentious quality about the Flyover way of life, where people really are what they seem and the only things people brag about are how many grandkids they have and the size of the fish they caught. The East and West Coasts are currently obsessed with understatement and simplicity in home decorating, fashion, and lifestyle, but they got it from Flyover Nation. Flyover has recently brought back masculinity and femininity too.

American Christian culture has been under attack for longer than just the recent decades of our lives. Our faith-based freedom has been holding strong against a constant erosion of value and morality. The other day while watching *The Hobbit: The Battle of the Five Armies*, as Thranduil lost his steed—and instead of losing his head, outnumbered in a battle with the Orcs, fought against them fluidly, slaying two at a time—I happened to glance at my sons' school portraits and wondered if I should have more children just to raise up a tiny army of little Christian conservatives to push back. The Left is so very clever.

Whether it's an intended effect or not, you can't help but recognize how beautifully all of their efforts have dovetailed into one magnificent weapon. First a rot crept into the hearts of some men and they viewed women the opposite of how God commanded in Scripture. Instead of loving them as Christ loves His church, they took them for granted, and in our country a faction of these men withheld from women the equality that was granted to them by God. In Ephesians 5:25–27 men are told:

> *Husbands, love your wives, just as Christ also loved the church and gave Himself up for her, so that He might sanctify her, having cleansed her by the washing of water with the word, that He might present to Himself the church in all her glory, having no spot or wrinkle or any such thing; but that she would be holy and blameless. So husbands ought also to love their own wives as their own bodies. He who loves his own wife loves himself; for no one ever hated his own flesh, but nourishes and cherishes it, just as Christ also does the church, because we are members of His body.*

Men are called to sacrifice for their wives and held to account otherwise. Make no mistake, that dragon of evil as described in Revelation is always creeping about, exploiting every transgression as a way to further drive a wedge between mankind and God. It's for this reason that I have Ephesians 6:12–13 tattooed on my arm.

It was Democrats who tried to rob women[139] of the dignity and equality given to us by God—not man—just as it was Democrats who sent Native Americans on the trail of genocide, disarmed the free men in the South, and filibustered against the Civil Rights Act; this same party, which so often carries that seed of division, has found itself on the wrong side of every issue in American history. At some point they attempted a rather brilliant about-face, so far as optics are concerned. Progressivism swept through their ranks when pro-life suffragettes such as Susan B. Anthony and Elizabeth Cady Stanton were lost to history and less accomplished women with questionable agendas took their place. The grandmothers of the feminist movement would not recognize the movement for women's rights today. Progressivism whispered into women's ears that their nurturing hearts, capable bodies, and fierce family loyalty were remnants of a bygone era of patriarchal oppression. Women rightfully resented having to fight to vote, and yet progressivism persuaded them to side with the people who had fought for over forty years to deny them the right to vote. With the fracture in the male-female relationship achieved, progressivism worked its way through the American family (simply murder your babies as birth control until you're ready to accept the responsibility that comes with engaging in the act of intercourse) and into the American economy. If it was beneath a woman to stay at home with her family, then the economy will surely make it so that she can't afford to choose freely. I'm always amazed that the party of prochoice does all it can to limit women's choice in every respect, from the economic freedom to choose to visiting a community health center to even obtaining birth control over the counter. Here Republicans have pushed for over-the-counter birth control and the Left opposes it. Now that the economy is in shambles, the American family is on the decline, and faith is openly ridiculed, it's the perfect time to finish it off, finish off that shining city on a hill, finish off the American dream.

With the help of their new god, Mother Nature, the coastals now have a plan for how they can do it.

CHAPTER 9

Conserving What We Have

Growing up in the country, I didn't have to go on a field trip or watch some documentary on TV to know that the natural world around me was special. Nobody had to explain that to me. I learned it on my own.

I received my education on the natural world from the creek beds and tree branches, the open fields, and cloistered valleys. Some of my earliest memories involve my cousins and me running free in the woods where my family lived—as elementary schoolers! We used to wake up in the mornings, eat breakfast, and pack bags full of water, compasses, Band-Aids, snacks, and pocketknives and set out deep into the woods on the hunt for the elusive Bigfoot. Sometimes we'd get lucky and come across a doe. Once we came across a copperhead and expertly navigated around it, as we could identify poisonous snakes and berries, and we knew not to eat mushrooms without asking Grandpa about them first. Sometimes we chalked tree trunks as we walked through the woods to note something of interest in the area, like a hidden cave or animal den. The creeks and clearings in the rolling hills of southern Missouri served as our classroom and playground. We'd dash through the woods and out into a sun-soaked meadow, playing freeze tag, dodgeball, or our made-up game called simply "war," where we cousins would divide and wage combat with one another all over Grandma and Grandpa's front yard—all games surely dismissed by today's progressive parents as too violent or reminiscent of actual combat. We'd go until our little legs simply ran out of juice and we collapsed, happy and exhausted, into the grass. Our only regret was killing Grandma's weeping willow, an old, enormous tree that once occupied most of her front yard. That poor tree endured numerous children climbing up its trunk and swinging on its branches as we pretended we were Tarzan.

Our family used to take us to Black River, where we would congregate on the riverbank. The adults would listen to music, drink beer, and make up for lost time together; we kids would build elaborate holding systems in the sides of the riverbank for all of the tadpoles and crawdads we caught. We'd examine the tadpoles at various stages of their development; some had leg buds, some had full-on legs, some had neither. We grouped them accordingly. After a long day at the river we'd pile into the back of my uncle's pickup truck (no seatbelts!) on the way back to Grandma and Grandpa's house. Towels draped over our shoulders, drinking Capri Suns, the wind drying our hair as we traveled through the lush green farmland and the sun's rays waned over the hills; sometimes we'd lie in the back of the pickup's bed and see who could find the most imaginative shapes in the clouds. We'd fill our lungs with good, clean air—air somehow never tastes better than it does when you're young and alive and living in God's country. *That*, that was joy. Somehow I knew it then, that moments like these would grow scarcer as I grew older. The sky would fade to orange and purple, and as the first shadows cast themselves across our faces, we'd get the message that the world was sending and get up to head home, where Grandma always had a hot meal and bath waiting. The memories of my childhood are tinted with a golden eighties hue, like the dying sun at the end of a long day at the river.

One of the simplest and most brilliant books ever written is Dr. Seuss's *Oh, The Places You'll Go!* I bought this book for the first time to read to my toddlers, and the last lines got to me. It's opener there in Flyover Nation, in the wide-open air.

Throughout this book I've been arguing that most of the beliefs held by the people who run this country have no basis in reality. Geography created their ignorance. No issue taps into this divide so clearly as our feelings about the environment. There are people who would sneer at these sorts of recollections. They might dismiss them as "quaint" and "provincial" as they huddle in their corner of Starbucks or sit crammed on a crowded subway car. I pity them. I pity that they never knew such unencumbered freedom in their youth. I pity that they've never known such happy simplicity. I can't imagine my childhood any differently. Let them dismiss away. Deep down, they're probably just jealous. (And if they've bought this book, the joke's on them anyway.) But anyone who comes from the land of real America knows exactly what I'm talking about. This will resonate with them. The sheer, unbridled joy of unsupervised time outside is one of the hallmarks of a childhood in Flyover Nation. It was one of the aspects of my own childhood that I loved the best, and one that I work very hard to pass along to my own children. Whenever the weather is nice and I don't have to be in the studio, we find a way to get outside—even if it's just for a walk, an hour on the zip line in the backyard, a couple hours at the range, or a half hour at the park. Of course, these days usually the laptop or smartphone ends up tagging along, keeping us at least somewhat connected to, not to mention distracted by, the world of work. This technology that was not nearly as accessible to me growing up as a free-roaming kid (our cell phones were the size of bricks— *bricks*—and they flipped) is now just part of the territory for millions of working parents. What matters is that I'm able to get out of the house or the office or the studio and spend some time with my kids out in the fresh air.

Kids learn from what they see, and what I saw growing up was adults who spent time outside. My grandfather was a farmer who dealt with cattle; in fact, many members of my family farmed. They knew to respect, and how to care for, the land. It's something ingrained in our family, though I'm not sure to what I'd attribute it. My family has always had an association with the land; my grandfather explained that if you respect the land, the land respects you. Don't overgraze. Let the land rest every few years. Care for your animals. Don't hunt to the point where it harms herd health. Abusing the land and its wildlife carries with it an even bigger consequence beyond bad stewardship: It may mean no meat for your family's freezer next winter, no vegetables on your table the coming summer, no fall harvest. For people who prefer to omit the middle man and harvest their meat and vegetables from nature, it means your family might go hungry.

My great-grandfather was a farmer, and his father before him. Before them part of my family was settled in a different part of the United States; some of my ancestors were removed by Jackson's soldiers during the Trail of Tears. During one family reunion a great-aunt once pointed out death records of ancestors whose untimely end was noted as being on the trail by those overseeing their brutal forcible relocation. (I always joke about how the "esteemed" senator from Massachusetts, Elizabeth Warren, has ancestors who rounded up mine. That is the closest she comes to actual American Indian ethnicity, say genealogists.) My grandfather was a poor farmer whose nickname was a racial slur, not maliciously meant, that stuck with him throughout his life (and even in the town's phone book and on his headstone) due to his beautiful golden brown skin. I was always proud of our ancestry, though it was more immediate to my grandparents than it was to me. We are so blessed in these United States to live in the middle of such a diverse ecosystem. We are blessed with lakes and streams and rivers—not to mention oceans—along with plains and grasslands, forests filled with hundreds of kinds of trees, and mountains that scrape the sky. Nearly every kind of climate you can think of can be found within our borders, along with myriad creatures that walk, crawl, fly, and swim within them.

Native Americans understood how critical it was to live in harmony with the natural world. That's a mentality I share today and strive to share with my children. Actually, it's shared by many in Flyover Nation, where we generally live closer to the land than do our counterparts in the concrete plains or glass-and-steel canyons of our coastal urban centers. We understand that as the top-functioning species on earth, we humans do need to work to be good stewards of our natural habitat.

You might read that and think it makes me an environmentalist. You would be wrong. It makes me a conservationist, and there's an important distinction. Conservationists believe in living in harmony with the land that sustains us. We practice the basic philosophy of "waste not, want not" to conserve our natural resources. Environmentalists, on the other hand, are a quasireligious sect of nut-eating hemp wearers and will turn swaths of California farms into desert wastelands over a stupid minnow. They believe not that humanity should live in balance with nature but that humans are a plague dedicated single-mindedly to destroying the paradise of planet Earth by any means necessary. They do not include humans in their equation about nature.

There are a few ways to tell the difference between conservationists and environmentalists—their preferred habitats, for one. Environmentalists are usually found on the coasts in dense cities that were built on shipping American goods abroad (and now specialize in shipping American jobs abroad). Some can be found scattered elsewhere around the country, holed up in colleges and universities, high up in ivory towers where they can send down an acid rain of moralizing judgments and proclamations about how awful humans are for this planet. You can also spot them in airports on their way to and from Very Important International Conferences about the dangers of fossil fuels . . . traveling on airplanes that burn fossil fuels. Wherever there is no one growing anything or making anything, there will be plenty of environmentalists.

Conservationists, on the other hand, can be found in the Flyover Nation. We appreciate the land not because some washed-up presidential wannabe told us we should. We don't believe with cultlike devotion the alarmist mantras that the world is dying and it's all our fault and we're all terrible people if we don't drive hybrid cars. We don't go in for those kinds of hysterics in general. We don't need to be seen tearing our hair out over gases in the atmosphere or this or that endangered species to claim our place in some celebrity outrage culture.

We do, however, love our fields and streams—our hiking, our swimming, our hunting, and our fishing. We grew up on the land and want to preserve it for our children and our children's children, but we want to do so in our own way, as individuals and groups and communities. We don't need Washington sending out top-down edicts telling us how to do it or forcing us to do it with unnecessary regulations. We've seen Washington's abysmal track record when it comes to actually keeping land and water safe and the totally rancid culture of the top agency tasked with this mission. In fact, the only thing the federal bureaucrats "responsible" for the environment seem to be good at—especially in the Obama administration—is destroying American jobs left and right.

That's because this isn't really about the environment for them, or for the leftist president they serve, or for the leftist academics and "green business" executives and activists who form the president's base of support. For them the main concern is not even the land itself but the advancement of their ideology.

In Washington "the environment" is purely a political issue. It's used by people to make money or push a socialist agenda under the pretense of caring for our trees, lakes, and cute furry animals. Being "green" is big business—as umpteen companies supported by the Obama administration demonstrated with our tax dollars before going belly up. The new snake oil is "carbon credits."

It's a matter of faith for them, and those of us in Flyover Nation—the conservationists, who genuinely appreciate the land for its own sake and not for political or monetary gain—

are viewed as apostates by members of the First Church of Environmentalism.

But when they put their faith in government institutions like the EPA, it shows how far gone they truly are.

The shopping mall lives on in Flyover Nation. I understand that on the coasts the majority of shopping must be done in tiny, overpriced boutiques where everything is hand-fashioned and crafted with sustainable materials (not to mention gluten/GMO/dairy/soul-free) and put into the ever-present hemp bag. Or everything is bought online, which doesn't even require leaving the house. But where I'm from we still go to Walmart, Kroger, and, yes, the mall. Admittedly, I prefer to buy online simply because I hate being presented with so many choices upon walking into the store. I buy black T-shirts and black jeans in bulk and have four pairs of black boots. Even my sneakers are black. I don't hate the mall; I rather like the concept of it. In some areas, however, the malls are barely hanging on. They lose a lot of their stores, and the ones that replace them seem to get seedier and seedier as you move through the complex, to the point where you don't really want to take the kids there anymore, much less let them go by themselves. Malls are closing down altogether all across America, in yet another sign of the "Obama recovery."

A shopping mall with shuttered, dingy storefronts could also stand as a representation for Obama's Washington. As you move through the streets of America's capital, you pass federal agency after federal agency, each its own engine of regulation and factory of bureaucratic red tape that makes things tougher on normal Americans. Just like the storefronts at a neglected shopping mall, each agency is seemingly worse than the last. And then, around the corner, you see it: the worst store in a bad mall. In Washington the worst agency in that bureaucracy-crazy town is the laughably named Environmental Protection Agency.

A product of the environmental movement and the general hippiedom of the 1960s, the EPA was created by the decidedly unhippie President Richard Nixon in 1970 in order to "effectively ensure the protection, development and enhancement of the total environment itself,"[140] as Nixon said in his message to Congress about the agency's creation. That's not a bad goal in and of itself—in fact, it even kind of sounds more conservationist than environmentalist; the mistake was a federal rather than state-level creation. To accomplish the stated goal, Nixon envisioned "pulling together into one agency a variety of research, monitoring, standard-setting and enforcement activities now scattered through several departments and agencies."[141] Increasing government to "streamline" it and make it more efficient never works. Predictably, like all big government agencies, once the EPA was up and running, it fell into the standard Washington pattern of gobbling up as much power as it possibly could and not being afraid to wield it. Federal agencies seem to view their regulatory and "enforcement" authority with an attitude along the lines of "If you don't use it, you lose it," and the EPA is no exception. Now, as it approaches its fiftieth anniversary, the EPA has built up a legacy of mismanagement, overreach, bullying, and just plain cluelessness—all of which have carried dire consequences, often for Flyover folks. (Said Dr. Robert Gwadz of the National Institutes of Health: "The ban on DDT may have killed 20 million children."[142])

According to Dr. Mark Hendrickson of Grove City College, who has studied the EPA's history of "misfeasance and malfeasance, misdeed, and mischief" for decades, even the agency's early years were fraught with suspicious activity. In 1972, for instance, just two years into the EPA's life, its first administrator, William Ruckelshaus, decided to ban DDT, a pesticide known mostly for cutting down on mosquitoes in American communities. The problem, however, was that Ruckelshaus made his decision in the face of "several hundred technical documents and testimony of 150 scientists," which, according to Dr. Hendrickson, led the judge who examined the DDT case for the EPA to conclude that it was likely not harmful to humans.[143] Ruckelshaus decided to ignore the scientific recommendations and banned DDT anyway—for political reasons, of course—and in doing so established a strong precedent of overreach by the EPA to score ideological points.

Just a few years later Congress was forced to deal with another example of the EPA's willingness to mislead in order to achieve ideological ends. In 1978 the agency proposed new standards for air quality that would have imposed significant costs on businesses. Of course, the EPA was not especially eager to have the true cost of its regulations exposed. According to Dr. Hendrickson, the EPA tried to keep the cost estimates of its proposed red-tape bonanza quiet—and it would have gotten away with it too, if not for two Republican senators from Pennsylvania, John Heinz and Richard Schweiker. They stymied the EPA's efforts in order to protect jobs in their home state. Had the new regulations been allowed to proceed, they would have, in Dr. Hendrickson's opinion, "effectively shut down the U.S. steel industry."[144] Early on, the EPA displayed a callous disregard for the impact of its actions on actual American workers—you know, the ones who *don't* work in comfy Washington government offices—which has not lessened with time.

The next decades saw plenty of similar scandals. Outside scientists tasked with a review of the EPA in 1991 found much to be desired, accusing the agency of making its science work for its own purposes. The administrator at the time, William Reilly, even admitted that "scientific data have not always been featured prominently in environmental efforts and have sometimes been ignored even when available."[145] That's not something you want to hear from someone whose job it is to use taxpayer dollars to come up with good scientific data. A few years later, in 1993, the problem had still not gone away, prompting Michigan representative John Dingell—a Democrat—to compare the EPA's approach to science with disreputable accounting. The agency "cooks the books with great vigor," Dingell said.[146] Carol Browner, the EPA administrator under Bill Clinton, ran the agency like a tinhorn dictator— keeping analytic practices secret, breaking federal lobbying laws, and even demanding that the City of San Diego stop treating its own sewage in order to protect "sewage-based ecology."[147] And yet the agency keeps chugging along.

Fast-forward to today, when Barack Obama's EPA has shown no signs of improvement—and really, no signs that it deserves to stay in existence. The agency continues to be riddled with what Congress's top investigator characterized in 2015 as "glaring management failures," including "numerous examples of fraud, unprofessional behavior, cronyism and outright theft."[148] In one bizarre case in 2013, an EPA official stole some $900,000 while claiming that he was "working undercover for the CIA" to cover himself at the office. Another employee was found to have preyed on at least seventeen women with "conduct and exchanges considered to be unwelcome," which, according to the Associated Press, included "unwelcome touching, hugging, kissing and photographing of women."[149] The AP noted that one of the women involved was just twenty-one, an intern at the Smithsonian. To round things out, a recent report by the agency's inspector general also cited multiple instances of employees discovered watching pornography at work.[150] Your tax dollars at work, ladies and gentlemen.

Obama's EPA troubles began early. The first EPA head under the Obama administration, Lisa Jackson, resigned during a storm of scandal in December 2012. Both congressional investigators and the EPA's own inspector general had launched investigations into her use of a private, unofficial e-mail account to conduct official government business (sound familiar?). Jackson was apparently using the e-mail alias "Richard Windsor" to communicate with her staff.[151] Hardly a model of open government, especially on the watch of a president who declared just a few months later that he was leading "the most transparent administration in history."[152]

We'll all have to make sacrifices to save the earth, say the coastals, by which they mean *you* all have to make sacrifices.

Barack Obama likes to call his administration the most transparent, in spite of the actions of his first EPA administrator and his secretary of state, to name just two. What's *very* transparent is that his administration has certainly been one of the most ideologically motivated in history. As a product of the radical Left, Barack Obama made no secret of his own leanings— strictly environmentalist, not conservationist. Remember, this was the man who cited his own nomination for president as "the moment when the rise of the oceans began to slow and our planet began to heal."[153]

He also laid out how we were going to get there, and a big part of that was bankrupting the coal industry. In 2008, in an interview with the editorial board of the *San Francisco Chronicle*, then-Senator Obama described his intention to aggressively pursue regulation of carbon emissions.

"So if somebody wants to build a coal-powered plant, they can," he explained. "It's just that it will bankrupt them, because they're going to be charged a huge sum for all that greenhouse gas that's being emitted."[154] Since he couldn't just unilaterally shut down the evil coal companies, the plan was to effectively starve them out of existence with regulation and fees—and starve the middle class, who rely on affordable and plentiful energy, in the process.

It looks like that plan is working—just ask the tens of thousands of American workers who on Obama's watch lost their jobs that were once supported by the coal industry. This disturbing trend surfaced early on. In December 2009, less than a year after Obama took office, CONSOL Energy announced that it would have to lay off some five hundred workers in West Virginia. CONSOL was in the midst of a lawsuit brought by the Sierra Club and other environmentalist groups. At the time, Obama's EPA was slow-walking nearly eighty mining permits around the country. CONSOL's CEO, Nicholas Deluliis, blamed the job cuts in part on "a constant stream of activism in rehashing and reinterpreting permit applications that have already been approved or . . . inequitable oversight of our operations."[155] Things only got worse from there. In June 2014 the *Washington Times* reported that "coal mines are closing down so rapidly in the wake of a raft of federal environmental regulations targeting coal that mining employment is now in a 'free fall.'" The *Times* cited a report by the research firm SNL Energy that was based on the government's own data. SNL found that jobs in the mining industry had dropped 8.3 percent between March 2013 and March 2014.[156]

The next year brought more grim news. In February 2015 a comprehensive report by the American Action Forum revealed that between 2008 and 2013, essentially the first half of the Obama administration, power plants cut nearly 40,000 jobs and coal mines shed more than 3,700 workers. According to the Bureau of Labor Statistics—government data—coal jobs dropped by an additional 4,800 between January 2014 and January 2015.[157] The American Action Forum blamed the job losses on overzealous federal regulation, with the EPA leading the charge. It noted that coal mines and power plants had been slapped with additional federal red tape that had cost the industries more than $10 billion since 2011.[158]

Let's take a step back from the numbers and look at the people behind them. Let's look at *where* these jobs in the mining industry are found—or at least *were* found before the Obama administration got rid of them. The SNL report from 2014 notes central Appalachia fared the worst, losing 15 percent of its mining jobs in the previous year.[159] The American Action Forum report was even more specific. For instance, it found that the four states with the most jobs lost at power plants were Kentucky, West Virginia, Ohio, and Pennsylvania.[160]

In other words, these jobs are disappearing from Flyover Nation. Obama's EPA and its "war on coal" has left our communities decimated. According to the *Wall Street Journal*, unemployment rates in coal-rich areas of the nation are abysmal—8 percent in eastern Kentucky and more than 10 percent in southern West Virginia.[161] And that doesn't even count the laid-off or retired coal workers who could stand to lose what benefits they still get if regulations eventually force their companies to go bankrupt.

These workers in mines and power plants are fathers, brothers, mothers, and sisters. They have families to support in an economic climate that is already making it tough for working families to catch a break. Entire communities depend on coal mines and power plants to provide the jobs that sustain them, and those are the places that are being hurt by the Obama EPA.

But Barack Obama doesn't care. He's made it plain that the hardships of Flyover communities don't merit his time or attention. After all, these were the kinds of backwaters where, as he put it, "bitter" people "cling to guns or religion." It's awfully easy to direct your EPA to starve an entire industry to death as part of an ideological environmentalist crusade when you don't know or care about any of the people who are going to lose their jobs as a result. If the coal plants that were hemorrhaging jobs under the Obama administration were located in San Francisco or Brooklyn, the EPA would probably be taking a different approach.

CHAPTER 10

Our Leaders Hate Us

You could literally smell the tourists coming into the Capitol.
—Senate leader Harry Reid, on Americans

Nobody likes a crybaby. Especially if he's a sixty-five-year-old adult male who happens to be in the third-most-powerful office in America and beats his face on every surface in his bathroom while misusing exercise bands (a new phrase for "mafia beating"—I kid! Don't delete it, legal!). But there was Tang-colored former Speaker of the House John Boehner weeping like he'd just lost his favorite golf club as he announced his resignation from Congress. You see, mean old conservatives kept trying to get him to challenge the president and do what millions of people elected his party to do in a 2014 landslide.

But shed no tears for John Boehner. He's almost certain to go the way of other disgraced politicians—cashing in on their time in office to make millions of dollars so they can stay as far away from Flyover Nation as possible. Make no mistake: John Boehner has total contempt for the millions of Americans who supported the Tea Party and constitutional conservatives. He said as much when he resigned, blasting those "who whip people into a frenzy" to do things that "are never going to happen." Crazy ideas like reducing the size of government, repealing Obamacare, cutting spending—positions supported by a vast majority of Americans.

In the end, Boehner has no interest in supporting the folks who elected him. And neither did his close friend and colleague Eric Cantor, who was booted out of Congress in the biggest upset in more than a century. Cantor, who worked against his own constituents on a host of issues, turned right around after being fired by them to prove just how right about him they had been. The man accused of being a candidate of Wall Street, not Main Street, went right to work for—wait for it—a Wall Street investment firm! He's now employed as vice chairman of Moelis & Company, where, the *Washington Post* reported, he will make twenty-six times the average salary of people in his former district.[162]

Don't get me wrong, I'm a capitalist. I'm not some street-defecating hippie occupying Wall Street. Just because they are rich doesn't mean our elected representatives can't understand us, but it does make it harder to sympathize with the ordinary struggles of the working class—because they don't remember them. They don't even really live in Flyover country anymore—or even in the states they claim to revere and represent in Washington. Look how many of them, when their jobs no longer require them to live with the coastals, choose to stay. When they have a choice, they spend as little time around us unwashed masses as possible. They do so only as a vote-getting vehicle.

Take Speaker Boehner, for example: After weeping over the

fine folks of his district in Ohio, who put their faith in him and elected him to office thirteen times, he announced plans to retire to an $850,000 condo in beautiful Cleveland. *Not.* He's actually going to live with other fat cats in a "luxury residence" in Marco Island, Florida, where the average household is worth over $650,000. That is, when Boehner isn't jetting back to DC to reap millions as a lobbyist from his years of "public service." See ya later, Ohio! Waving good-bye to Flyover country in the rearview mirror is a bipartisan epidemic. In 2014 a Kansas senator almost lost his job when his constituents learned he no longer lived in Kansas. That's right—Pat Roberts, a creature/caricature of the political establishment, owned no home or apartment in the state he was elected to serve. His primary residence was in a suburb of Washington, DC—suburbs that are quickly becoming filled with senators, congressmen, ex-senators, ex-congressmen, and lobbyists, to become among the wealthiest in America.

Richest Counties in America[163]		
	County	Median Household Income
1	City of Falls Church, VA	$121,250
2	Loudoun County, VA	$118,934
3	Los Alamos County, NM	$112,115
4	Howard County, MD	$108,234
5	Fairfax County, VA	$106,690
6	Hunterdon County, NJ	$103,301
7	Arlington County, VA	$99,255
8	Douglas County, CO	$98,426
9	Stafford County, VA	$95,927
10	Somerset County, NJ	$95,574
11	Morris County, NJ	$95,236
12	Montgomery County, MD	$94,365
13	Prince William County, VA	$93,011

Senator Roberts admitted that he didn't occupy his former home in Kansas and preposterously claimed he slept on a friend's recliner whenever he visited his (former) state.[164] Which probably tells you how many nights the seventy-nine-year-old actually spends in Kansas. The now-former Indiana senator Richard Lugar used to rent hotel rooms when he went home to visit with constituents in Indiana, the state that elected him. And he listed an address on his voter registration card where he did not live. At one point the Lugars actually were informed they were not even residents of the state.[165] Mary Landrieu of Louisiana was labeled "the Senator from Washington, DC," because she spent so much time working for the rich denizens of the District, where she actually lived in a $2.5 million home, than in the state of Louisiana, where she only pretended to live.[166]

She, like so many politicians claiming to care about Flyover country, is literally phoning it in. And where do most of them spend their time? Places like the Ritz-Carlton Residences, where Senator Harry Reid, the Democratic Party's majority leader and professional poor-mouther, lives next to former Democratic Party leader Tom Daschle and a number of other Washington big shots. Asked about his residence, Senator Reid made it sound like any old low-cost housing. "I live in a one-bedroom apartment," he insisted.[167] That one-bedroom apartment comes with access to housekeeping, valet parking, private chefs, and a posh health club and spa. The Web site for the residence simply calls it "Life at the Top."[168] Yep, just like every ordinary American.

Flyover is different.

My grandparents had a giant bug zapper that hung on their front porch. On summer nights I'd sit out there, looking over the

Astroturfed front porch and sipping iced tea—and, once I got older, stronger beverages—and watching bugs fly to their deaths. The moths, June bugs, and mosquitoes would buzz and hum lazily around the porch, pulled in toward the light by forces they couldn't control, drawn closer and closer by its glow. Then I'd hear the sound of an electric bolt zapping their life away like Sith lightning. In the stillness of those quiet nights, the cacophony of death and discovery was a comforting sound. Some evenings we would sit in silence, watching the insect tragedies play out, but other evenings we would talk. Sometimes I'd listen to the most serious gossip, which occurred after the sun went down, as though the darkness muffled sound and eliminated sight. I remember a lot of the conversations we had on that porch. My grandparents could always be relied upon for a plain, unvarnished helping of country wisdom, and they had a knack for cutting through fluff and getting straight to the heart of an issue. Growing up, I knew I could come to them with any problem. Grandma was my fierce advocate. She knew I hated living in the city during the week and that I felt alone. Grandpa rarely spoke but when he did, it was to say either something hysterical or something so insightful that you could feel the weight of the wisdom. Our porch talks always helped me better understand the world around me. Every now and then, I'd get a lesson on politics in our local community—how mayors are elected, how a police force is formed and run, and other insights into town government. An uncle was a deputy, so-and-so was the mayor of the tiny town, which was insane that it even had enough people and administrative responsibilities for a mayor to handle). Sometimes we'd get to talking about other levels of government too. Grandpa rarely minced his words, and he knew just what to say when the conversation turned to the federal government and Washington, DC.

"In a way," he once said, looking toward the glowing light that had just claimed another moth, "that bug killer is like Warshington." (Where we're from, people pronounce an *r* in "wash." I'm not even going to apologize. I also say "pellow" for "pillow" and "melk" for "milk.") "That light attracts people, even the good people, and it kills 'em."

At first I wasn't quite sure what Grandpa meant. Like, they're *literally* zapped by Washington? But as I grew up and came to have more experience with government and the people who run it, his simple comparison between the capital of the free world and your standard, garden-variety Walmart bug zapper came to make a lot of sense. It wasn't as comforting a thought as the bug-zapper sound, either. Washington folks, whether they're elected officials or unelected bureaucrats, find themselves so drawn in to the toxic culture of that town, and before they even realize it, what humanity they had has been zapped away as if it were no more than a wayward mosquito.

Fitting, isn't it? Mosquitoes breed in swamps, after all—and legend has it that Washington, DC, itself was built on a swamp. Finicky historians can argue about the accuracy of this point—one says the idea simply stuck around "because it's such a useful analogy for the way Congress works,"[169] and another thinks the city's builders "were looking for a reason to explain why . . . development was so slow."[170] Either way, the metaphor holds.

Ronald Reagan certainly believed it. In January 1982, after his first year in the White House, he reminded his staff: "You're here to drain the swamp."[171] Politicians of all parties have been promising to do just that for years, vowing to do things differently, all the way up to President Obama, who, let's remember, essentially ran his entire campaign on two words: "hope" and "change." And yet for all the draining, all the hope, and all the change, the swamp remains.

Anyone who's spent an oppressively hot summer's day in Washington—and I don't recommend it—would swear they were smack in the middle of a muggy bog. The atmosphere of the place is heavy—heavy with the weight of stacks and stacks of regulations that seem to be much of the government's reason for existing, heavy with the hot air spouted nonstop by those whose idea of work is talking down to the rest of us, heavy with the self-importance that comes from spending so much time insulated in a marble bubble that's completely out of touch with the rest of the country.

That's not to say there aren't some decent people in Washington. I'm sure there are. The guy who works the night shift vacuuming the floors of government buildings or gleaming corporate offices can feel satisfied at having done an honest day's work. So can the lady who arrives early in the morning to set up her hot dog stand, which will feed hungry tourists making the desultory trek along the National Mall. And, of course, legions of police officers and other first responders work tirelessly every day to safeguard the lives of everyone in the city, from politicians to tourists to locals—like the cop who gave me a bottle of water one hot August day as I was covering a rally at the Lincoln Memorial and was about to drop.

But, regrettably, these aren't the people who run Washington. "We the People" don't run the place either, no matter what politicians of any party tell you. The dirty secret is that Washington is run by career politicians, entrenched bureaucrats, and corporate and special-interest lobbyists who are all pulling toward the same goal: keeping their own jobs as secure (and lucrative) as possible.

If you're interested in spotting these rare creatures in their natural habitat, you need to go where the real business is done in Washington. It's not in the Capitol, that gleaming temple of democracy that sometimes seems more like a taxpayer-funded country club. It's not even in the conference rooms of K Street, the enclave of high-powered lobbyists that's also been known as "Gucci Gulch." To see the real deals being struck—to see "how the sausage is made"—you need to go to places where there's actually meat on the menu. The real centers of power in Washington are the city's steakhouses, of which there is a seemingly endless supply. A DC food writer once quipped: "Want to see some Washingtonians go ballistic? Just call the District a 'steakhouse town,' a place where the natives' love of politics is rivaled only by their lust for thick slabs of charbroiled beef."[172]

Because I'm all for making Washingtonians go ballistic whenever possible, I'm going to agree. It *is* a "steakhouse town," and it's at those places where the three groups that hold all the cards— elected officials, bureaucrats, and lobbyists—come together to hatch their plots.

If you or I or anybody from the Flyover Nation were to somehow make it past the host or hostess—often the snootiest of the snooty—and take a peek into one of these places, we'd be met with an interesting scene. First of all, our eyes would have to adjust—it's always gloomy in those places, and the dark wood all over the place doesn't help. Then we'd start to notice details. There might be signed photos or drawings of dearly departed big shots on one wall and sealed wine lockers emblazoned with current high rollers' personalized nameplates on another. Huddled around the tables would be groups of mostly men—though women are just as capable of becoming members of the self-serving establishment—in dark suits, deep in conversation over wine or cocktails (beer is usually too "lowbrow" for these types).

Some in the group might be elected to represent the citizens of some far-flung Flyover Nation locale, some might be high-ranking officials in the president's administration, and some might take in great sums of money from major corporations, unions, or other special interests in order to advance their interests among the first two categories of Washington creature. Everyone around the table would have the same attitude: "Get along to go along." Keep the wheels of government moving "smoothly," keep the environment safe for Big Business, Big Labor, or whoever else has concerns, and keep the process as far away from the actual American people as humanly possible.

Eventually the meal itself would come out, but at your typical DC steakhouse it's almost an afterthought. That's right—in a town with so many steakhouses, it's actually hard to find a decent steak. A T-bone sizzling on any given grill in any given backyard on any given summer's day in Flyover Nation will beat an overcharred corporate DC sirloin anytime you please. I learned everything there is to know about grilling from my step-dad; any good backyard barbecue enthusiast could teach these DC chefs a thing or two. The best grilling is done during base-ball season, Jack Buck was the best audible seasoning, and you grill pork steaks, thick London broils, brats, and St. Louis–style ribs (cut with just enough fat on them to flavor the meat). Maybe if we fed these already overstuffed government and corporate folks some real American food—Flyover food—they'd have a come-to-Jesus moment and get on our side again. In any event, nobody at these confabs even cares what the food tastes like. Chances are it means nothing to them because they're not even paying for it; the firm or the clients are. Lobbying does not come cheap—it was a $3.24 billion industry in 2014. That year there were nearly twelve thousand registered lobbyists doing business.[173] Welcome to Washington.

Sitting down for expensive steak dinners with a side of cronyism several times a week is just one of the many ways Washingtonians make a point of keeping themselves apart from mainstream America, and particularly from Flyover Nation. To them we're just peasants, barely literate hicks who share a tooth and the same DNA, people whose proper role is to sit slack-jawed while the lords of the manor make their grand pronouncements from Capitol Hill or other assorted halls of power, then nod acceptingly—even gratefully!—when they've finished.

The saddest cases, though, are the folks who really did come to Washington with idealistic dreams of "making a difference." Some are born into it—you can often find the offspring or other relatives of elected officials working as lobbyists, as staffers, and elsewhere around town. But every year recent college graduates from all over the United States—Flyover Nation included—come to Washington for that first internship with dreams of changing the world. Maybe they all saw Frank Capra's inspiring—but hardly realistic—classic movie *Mr. Smith Goes to Washington*. More recent generations probably grew up on Aaron Sorkin's equally inspiring—and equally naive—television drama *The West Wing*. Something was kindled within them, a fire that burned brightly and illuminated what to them seemed like the true path: They must turn their passions into action, head to Washington, and fight for what they believe in.

So they head off to college and join campus political organizations. Student politics can be a heady experience for a kid from Flyover Nation, where politics really aren't discussed that much in polite company—frankly, we've got better things to talk about.

But most colleges today are inherently political environments. Idealistic kids engage in spirited debate with one another and with their teachers, cheering or booing (depending on affiliation) when the president makes a speech on television. After a few years of this, they leave with a degree in one hand—in political science, public policy, communications, or some such thing—and dreams in their hearts. They make tracks for Washington, DC, and when they show up they find . . . the swamp.

The find themselves in a land of sky-high rent and cost of living. Even the food is different. They can't afford the fancy steakhouses or the trendy GMO-free organic tapas places, and the canned chicken soup they buy doesn't taste anything like how Mom used to make it back home. Everyone they meet seems cagey, wary, sizing them up as potential competition. There is very little sense of community—genuine social gatherings take a backseat to soulless "networking events." The first thing out of any new acquaintance's mouth is a standard four-word phrase: "What do you do?" If your answer does not impress them, those will be the only words you hear—they'll be gone before your response is half over, moving on to someone more worth talking to. A kid from Flyover Nation might come to realize that Harry Truman was right: "If you want a friend in Washington," he said, "get a dog."

But these kids, exposed to the ways of Washington, don't automatically go running to local animal shelters. Instead they take one of two paths: Either they pack it in and go home (and arguably save themselves) or they start to change. The transition begins slowly, maybe in the way they talk or the jargon that slips into their e-mails home. Then differences in appearance emerge: Boys drop hefty amounts on a tailored suit for job interviews; girls' heels get a little bit higher. They start to play the game—learning which politicians are in favor, sizing up people as potential "contacts," and beginning to plot their next career move. Before long, they've scored an entry-level job and are well on their way to becoming a full-fledged DC denizen and leaving behind all traces of their Flyover roots. That's what my grandpa meant when he was talking about bugs getting drawn toward the zapper: "That light attracts people, even the good people, and it kills 'em." Washington does that to people, even good people. Once it sucks them in, they're usually stuck for good.

The longer anybody spends in Washington, the less contact they have with the real world. In 2014 Hillary Clinton—former First Lady, former U.S. senator, former secretary of state, and at that point still a not-quite candidate for president—dropped a telling revelation while addressing the National Association of Automobile Dealers.

"The last time I actually drove a car myself was 1996," she told her audience. She went on to turn it into a joke: "I remember it very well," she said. "Unfortunately, so does the Secret Service, which is why I haven't driven since then."

Of course this self-deprecating crack makes sense given the audience, but there is still some sweet irony about a politician—and a consummate one at that—making this sort of confession to a roomful of car dealers. But the kernel of truth within the joke—that Clinton hasn't driven a car herself in decades—shows the almost surreal alternate world the creatures of Washington inhabit.

How can someone who has been chauffeured across the country and around the world for nearly twenty years connect with a working mom in Flyover Nation? I can think of a lot of people who would just love to have a fleet of big black SUVs (gas-guzzlers, I might add) to take them to work, take their kids to school, pick the kids up and take them to basketball or gymnastics, and then hit the grocery store on the way home. Wouldn't that be nice? Alas, most of us can only dream of the rarefied existence enjoyed by the Hillary Clintons of the world. Hillary can laugh off the fact that she exists on an entirely different plane—if not a different planet—from her countrymen and countrywomen if she so desires. It's even possible to pity some of these politicians for being so divorced from reality. When was the last time the Clintons had a simple family dinner, or tossed a football around their yard, or even—God forbid—went to church together? And when was the last time any of these things were done with no cameras trained on them? Washington elites may have forgotten how to be real people, and that's their problem. A couple of years ago media reported that Hillary was asking her Hamptons friends for advice on how to reach out to the middle class. The Hamptons set was giving Hillary Clinton advice on how to talk economics to hardworking Flyover people.

What nobody should excuse, however, is when out-of-touch politicians in Washington come out of their own little fantasy world only to heap disdain upon the rest of us. They may have lived in DC so long that they simply don't "get" people from Flyover Nation, but that doesn't mean they can talk down to us. It doesn't mean they can demean whole groups of people who they feel are less entitled to enjoy the city of Washington than they are. It doesn't mean they can viciously insult someone trying to do her job who happened to get in their way. There's simple obliviousness, and then there's outright contempt. The nastiest characters in Washington are those with such high levels of the former that they feel compelled to belch forth examples of the latter.

Who exactly do I mean? Let's meet some of the worst offenders.

Harry Reid: Literally Holding His Nose

It was December 2, 2008, and Washington big shots were gathered on Capitol Hill for the grand opening of the Capitol Visitor Center. The massive underground facility, which sprawled to nearly 580,000 feet, was the largest addition ever to what official DC likes to call the "Capitol Complex" and was being dedicated on the 145th anniversary of the day that the *Statue of Freedom* was erected at the top of the Capitol dome.[174] In true Washington fashion, it had been completed way behind schedule and way over budget, taking four years and over $350 million more than expected, for a total cost of $621 million.[175] But that barely even counts as "real money" in Washington, and pesky considerations like that weren't going to spoil the pomp and dignity of the dedication ceremony.

Senate Majority Leader Harry Reid, Democrat of Nevada, was probably having a particularly good day. His party controlled both houses of Congress, and barely a month earlier the American people had chosen his party's candidate to be the forty-fourth president of the United States—a Senate colleague of Reid's named Barack Obama, who had not even served out his first full term. It was a good day to be a Democrat in Washington.

Maybe Senator Reid's pride in the afterglow of Obama's election and his gleeful anticipation of total Democratic control of the government got the better of him that day. Maybe that explains why he let his guard down when he took the podium and showed the audience a glimpse of his real self and what he thinks of the rest of us—his Nevada constituents, everyone in Flyover Nation, and the rest of the American people. When Reid got up to speak, he chose to praise the facility for its efficiency in getting "long lines" of visitors into the Capitol. He then proceeded to share why this was so important to him personally but began with a cautionary note: "My staff has always said, 'Don't say this,' but I'm going to say it again because it's so descriptive because it's true." Reid went on:

> In the summertime, because [of] the high humidity and how hot it gets here, you could literally smell the tourists coming into the Capitol. [Cue laughter from the crowd of Reid's fellow elites.] And that may be descriptive but it's true. Well, that is no longer going to be necessary.[176]

Suddenly, spending $621 million on a 580,000-square-foot bunker makes complete and total sense: At least the Senate majority leader wouldn't have his delicate nose offended by real people.

What kind of message does that send to the American kids who come to Washington, DC, to finally see with their own eyes the sights they've only read about in school? What does it say to the parents and teachers who guide them? What about the millions of Americans or visitors from foreign nations who come to our Capitol because they happen to be inspired by what it represents? Senator Reid told them simply: "Go home. You stink."

There were probably times in Harry Reid's life when he didn't smell so great himself. That can be a side effect of not having regular access to running water, and as Reid's official biography notes, he grew up "in the small rural mining town of Searchlight . . . in a small cabin without indoor plumbing."[177] His childhood was tough. Both parents drank—his father, a gold miner, committed suicide and his mother earned extra money by doing laundry for local brothels.[178] The schools in his hometown went up to only eighth grade, so Reid had to go to high school in the nearby town of Henderson. Local families gave him places to stay during the week, and when he graduated, Henderson businessmen helped pay for him to attend college at Utah State University.[179] After graduating in 1961, he headed for Washington, DC, for law school at George Washington University. While earning his law degree, he worked the night shift as a police officer at, of all places, the United States Capitol.[180] At least at night there probably weren't any smelly tourists around.

After law school Reid moved back to Henderson and became city attorney, touching off a political career that would include time in the Nevada State Assembly, becoming the state's youngest-ever lieutenant governor, and a stint on the Gaming Commission. His run at a job in DC failed when he lost a Senate race in 1974, but after his time on the Gaming Commission he tried for a House seat in 1982 and was successful. Winning election to the Senate in 1986, Reid has been the chamber's top Democrat—majority or minority leader—since 2005 and remains "indisputably the most powerful politician in Nevada—Democratic or Republican."[181]

Harry Reid came from humble beginnings—of which he seems to remain proud—and achieved success on the Nevada and national political stages. So what makes him think it's all right to look down on regular Americans who visit his place of work—the Capitol—as nothing more than foul-smelling inconveniences? Those "smelly tourists" own that building, you know. The answer may lie in the fact that along the path from the tiny cabin in Searchlight, Nevada, to the Senate Democratic leader's suite of offices in the Capitol, Reid's lifestyle changed big time.

When he first came to Washington in 1982, Reid's net worth was already at least $1 million, the *Las Vegas Review-Journal* reported.[182] It may have been even higher. Prior to 1982, while not serving in public office in Nevada—or serving only part time—Reid had continued to earn money by practicing law. Over the course of his career he has also made significant investments in real estate. This has helped his net worth reach an eventual peak of about $10 million, according to RealClearPolitics. Its analysis concludes that "Reid has walked a fine line over the years, occasionally breaking rules or engaging in brazenly unseemly behavior during his pursuit of wealth."[183] Some of the real estate deals that have helped enrich Harry Reid have raised ethical red flags. One involved a friend of Reid's named Jay Brown, who has variously been called a "master manipulator" (by a veteran Nevada political journalist)[184] and "always a person of interest" (by a retired FBI agent).[185] Reid invested $400,000 in some vacant land near Las Vegas and in 2001 transferred his stake to a company controlled by Brown. The problem: This transfer went unreported on Reid's financial disclosure forms. But that didn't stop him from collecting $1.1 million when Brown sold off the land in 2004—a profit of some $700,000.[186] Or there was the time that Reid's Senate priorities and private business interests happened to line up neatly around a town called Bullhead City in Arizona. Between 2004 and 2005 Reid—who had publicly supported earmark reform— pushed through an $18 million earmark to build a bridge between

Laughlin, Nevada, and Bullhead City, Arizona, situated across the Colorado River from each other.[187] A 160-acre plot of land in Bullhead City was owned by none other than Harry Reid himself—purchased from a friend a few years earlier at one tenth of its value, according to the *Los Angeles Times*.[188]

Reid hasn't just been clever in the real estate game. *National Review* reported that he sold off shares in the Dow Jones U.S. Energy Sector Fund, which includes major oil companies, in August 2008. A month later Reid helped pass legislation that, according to the Joint Committee on Taxation, would cost those companies "billions of dollars in taxes and regulatory fees." By early October the price of shares in the Energy Sector Fund had dropped 42 percent.[189] Reid's investments no doubt helped him purchase a home in Washington, where he is sure to remain unbothered by any tourist, stinky or otherwise. Since 2001 he has owned a condo in the Ritz-Carlton Residences in the fashionable West End area of downtown DC. Reid got in just a year after the building opened, and the value of his unit is currently estimated at around $1.1 million. His neighbors include his old pal from the Senate, Tom Daschle, along with a former UN ambassador, a former governor of Puerto Rico, and top lobbyists for Goldman Sachs and Toyota. A profile of the building— yes, you read that correctly—in *Politico*, a publication DC elites use to keep tabs on one another, explains what makes it so appealing to Reid and friends:

Indeed, the 162-unit, West End enclave . . . has gradually amassed a roster of Washington power brokers from politics, business and society. Which isn't that surprising considering its amenities: everything from Ritz-Carlton hotel services like room service, housekeeping, private

*chefs, valet parking, access to the Equinox Sports Club,
Cafe and Spa, 24-hour doorman security and proximity
to posh restaurants like Ris and the West End Bistro.*[190]

Just try to imagine this description read in the distinctive voice
of Robin Leach from the old TV show *Lifestyles of the Rich and
Famous.* Now remember that many of the "power brokers," like
Reid, who are enjoying their room service and valet parking are
supposed to be public servants. That makes it a lot less funny.

Reid's journey from a tiny shack in Searchlight, Nevada—
where he still has a home—to "DC's Tower of Power" was a
long one, helped along by his doing, as he put it in a 2010 debate,
"a very good job investing."[191] But nothing gives him the right to
dismiss those who come to Washington and *don't* stay at the
Ritz-Carlton as foul-smelling obstacles to his own enjoyment of
Capitol Hill. It's a sad sign of how far this miner's son has fallen
out of touch with Flyover Nation—and his own roots.

Chuck Schumer: Sit Down and Shut Up

Just because someone hails from Flyover Nation doesn't mean
they don't do plenty of flying themselves. These days plenty of
jobs require hopping on a plane and jetting around the country,
or even to elsewhere in the world. It's never fun to have to leave
your home and family, and the actual business of air travel itself
is not always an enjoyable experience. But when Flyover Nation
folks do travel, we remember the basic lessons of decency and
respect we were brought up with. These boil down to one rule
you might call, well, golden: "Do unto others as you would have
them do unto you." Common courtesy knows no boundaries,

and everyone deserves to be treated with respect, whether you meet them on land, at sea, or in the air.

Senator Chuck Schumer famously forgot this rule in December 2009. The New York Democrat was aboard a US Airways plane getting ready to take off for Washington—one of the short flights coastal types are fond of calling "the shuttle," often without specifying which city they're shuttling to (because if you can't figure it out, you're not important enough for them to be talking to). In this case Schumer and his fellow New York Democratic senator Kirsten Gillibrand were heading back to DC for crucial Senate business. President Obama was trying to shepherd his signature piece of legislation—the Affordable Care Act, commonly known as Obamacare—through Congress. Though both the House and Senate were held by Democrats, there were still points of contention about the bill, with some of the more committed liberals still angling for the inclusion of a "public option," a long-standing left-wing policy goal. Just a few weeks later, on Christmas Eve, the Senate would pass its version of Obamacare—with no public option—on a strict party-line vote. Schumer, Gillibrand, and every other Senate Democrat would vote for it, and every Republican against it.[192]

But as he waited for his flight to depart from LaGuardia Airport, Schumer found himself in a conflict more personal than political. Because he is a Very Important Politician, he was naturally jabbering away on his cell phone, probably talking to someone as important—or almost as important—as him. In the midst of his call, the pilot made the customary announcement that all cell phones needed to be switched off prior to takeoff. Schumer—because he is a Very Important Politician—naturally ignored this instruction, because such rules apply only to mere mortals. A flight attendant approached and asked him to turn his phone off, in accordance with the Federal Aviation Administration regulations that the vast majority of Americans observe and respect on thousands of flights every single day. Chuck Schumer's response, however, was to ask if he could finish his call. He could not, the flight attendant explained, because it was *his* phone that needed to be turned off before the aircraft could depart. He was holding up the entire flight.

Schumer was trapped. Perhaps he feared upsetting his fellow passengers, most of whom were almost certainly New York voters. Begrudgingly he turned off his phone. But he couldn't let the argument drop. Still intent on establishing his superiority over this insolent flight attendant, he proceeded to tell her that he actually should have been allowed to remain on the phone until the aircraft's door had been closed. The flight attendant handled this badgering from a U.S. senator very professionally. According to a witness: "She said she doesn't make the rules, she just followed them." With that, she walked away.[193] But Senator Schumer had to have the last word. When the flight attendant had left, he turned to Senator Gillibrand and growled: "B*tch!" The process of flying involves plenty of annoying rules. When you can sit, when you can stand, when you're supposed to take your shoes off at the airport, and, yes, when you have to hang up your phone. We all have to deal with them. Schumer, then the chairman of the Senate Rules Committee, thought that he didn't—because, as *New York* magazine later quipped, "he is Chuck Schumer and he's working on important things."[194] And he was so angry about it that he had to insult the person who simply informed him of an across-the-board rule.

A flight attendant's salary often starts as low as $25,000, and someone who has been on the job for a while can pull down as much as $50,000.[195] That's what they're paid to spend their days in a metal tube dealing with the demands of bored, uncomfortable, or disgruntled strangers. They must have the patience of saints and should be saluted for it. Dealing with tough customers is part of any job, in Flyover Nation and everywhere else, but a U.S. Senator should know better. Politicians, especially those with political-animal instincts as well honed as Schumer's, are supposed to have a folksy touch, right? A way with the "common people"? Maybe Schumer's patience with regular folks had already been exhausted by that point in the day. In any event, no woman should be called a "bitch"—by anyone—just for doing her job.

When I was growing up, there were always certain people in town who would get themselves talked about. Whether you'd talked to them recently or not, you always knew what they were up to. This kind of tendency is always more present in politicians, but Chuck Schumer seems to have taken it to a pathological level. He courts media attention with a zeal that impresses even his fellow DC personalities. Bob Dole, who served with Schumer in the Senate, said that "the most dangerous place in Washington is between Charles Schumer and a television camera."[196] President Obama himself once told a crowd of elites at a white-tie dinner in New York that he was glad to welcome Senator Schumer's "loved ones," adding, "Those would be the folks with the cameras and the notebooks in the back of the room."[197] In 2014 Schumer arranged for the news media to cover an especially momentous milestone in his Washington career—moving out of his house. Schumer had been living for more than thirty years in a townhouse on Capitol Hill with two other Democrats— Representative George Miller of California and Senator Dick Durbin of Illinois—in an arrangement that reportedly "inspired the Amazon web series 'Alpha House,' as well as countless punch lines about the crash pad's fraternity-meets-policy seminar vibe."[198] They also apparently paid around eight hundred dollars a month in rent while the average rent in DC when they moved out was nearly two thousand.[199]

Sensing that this was obviously something that was of serious world import, the roommates invited a *New York Times* reporter and an NBC camera crew to watch them move out. And they showed up. Only in DC would anyone think three late-middle-aged men finally moving on from the group-house life actually qualified as news. The *Times* gave it the full dramatic treatment, telling how "Mr. Schumer—his eyes moist—stood outside in the cold, clutching his comforter. 'I didn't realize that's when we'd be saying goodbye,' he said, suddenly serious. 'Whoa.'"[200] Whoa, indeed.

It's easy to see how someone who thinks spending a cold December morning moving stuff out of his house warrants national media coverage wouldn't take kindly to being put in his place by a flight attendant. But beyond his own armor of personal ego, Schumer's political allegiances might help explain his distaste for "common people."

Schumer is a known favorite of big banks. The top five donors over his political career read like a tour down Wall Street: Goldman Sachs, Citigroup, JPMorgan Chase, Credit Suisse, Morgan Stanley.[201] When Harry Reid announced his intention to retire in 2016 and Schumer was immediately touted as the favorite to replace him, CNN proclaimed this "welcome news to Wall Street." It called Schumer, a longtime member of the Senate Banking and Finance Committees, a "fierce champion" of the financial services industry who consistently supports its agenda and maintains "close personal relationships with many of New York's financial elite."[202] Coastal elites—even Democrats—always flock together. Maybe Schumer was on the phone to one of his banker pals when he was so rudely interrupted by a flight crew trying to take off. No wonder he thought he could get away with spitting venom at a flight attendant making a mere five figures. At least the publicity generated by Schumer throwing around the *b* word generated an apology, even if his office dismissed it in the same breath as "an off-the-cuff comment."[203] Interestingly, the *New York Post* reported that Schumer "has a reputation" among crews for being, in the words of one flight attendant, "not nice."[204]

To her immense credit, the flight attendant on the receiving end of Schumer's bad-mouthing on that December 2009 flight took the high road and accepted his apology. That was a move that took absolute class. It showed that she had been raised to show civility and respect even in the face of rudeness. Maybe she was raised in Flyover Nation.

Davos: Entitled Elitists Pretending to Care About the Poor

Where have the world's richest liberals decided is the best place to talk about global poverty? Why, Switzerland, of course, the richest, whitest, most expensive nation in the world. Between earnest talks about righting "income inequality"—a nonsense phrase that basically means taking money from successful people and giving it to losers—these do-gooders have plenty of time to hike the Alps or hobnob on their yachts. To most people in Flyover America, the World Economic Forum in Davos means nothing. They've never heard of it—and they're the lucky ones. Unfortunately what happens in Davos is a perfect example of why the world's elites are so out of touch with the rest of us.

Davos welcomes guilt-ridden rich people to sit around on panels, smile and nod, and pretend like they're saving the world. It's a place for people like Bill Clinton, America's professional groper-cum-gadfly, and his buddy Tony Blair to compare their latest iPhones and other trendy gadgets with celebrities, billionaires, and corporate criminals. One of the forum's "partners"—which shell out big bucks to these people so they won't be criticized by anyone—is the Kingdom of Saudi Arabia. The Saudis, of course, are notorious for caring about the rights of women—who are forbidden even to drive cars in their country. I'm sure they empathize with the world's poor—while spending millions to maintain their privileged lifestyles and keep as far away from the great unwashed as possible.

Yet together these people come up with all sorts of harebrained schemes to make America worse—fretting about taxing people more to solve "climate change" or explaining why we need to open the borders in America to every terrorist, cretin, or sad-sack failure with a dirty face and a sob story.

Luckily, thanks to the coastals' taste for solutionless solutions, they often come back from events like these feeling like the conference and resulting press conferences get the job done.

The rarefied world of receptions and dinners at high-end steakhouses has taken its toll, making them so far out of touch with real Americans that they get positively angry when they get in their way. Whether it's the smelly tourists ruining Reid's summers or a "bitch" flight attendant who dares to tell Schumer to follow the same rules as everyone else, it's clear they can't stand people like you and me. They are much more comfortable hobnobbing with their neighbors at the Ritz-Carlton Residences over room service or with their banker cronies on Wall Street. But the toxic environment that envelops Washington, DC, doesn't necessarily mean you should avoid it like the plague. This may go against your better judgment, but it's still a good place to visit. Why? Because seeing the monuments, the museums, and the buildings dedicated to the great American experiment still have the capacity to inspire. They may be populated by distasteful people who don't share—and actively hate—our Flyover values, but that doesn't mean we can't still appreciate what our capital city represents. Even the most hardened cynic still feels some pride looking up at Lincoln's marble gaze and reading the immortal words carved into the nearby wall—his pledge that "government of the people, by the people, for the people, shall not perish from the earth." Our government is bigger than some overfed, contemptuous politicians.

So take the kids to DC—just for a short trip. Soak up that pride in the American dream, and carry it home in your hearts. Because DC is not the heart of America—Flyover Nation is. And spare a thought for the folks you see scurrying in and out of the government buildings in Washington, the folks who've been there too long. Maybe they had dreams once too. They were like those bugs I saw droning toward the zapper on my grandparents' porch—they got sucked in and had the life zapped out of them.

Epilogue

I was on the first phone call and helped organize and found one of the first modern-day Tea Party groups in the United States. We were maligned, our characters impugned; we were called every name imaginable and referred to as racists simply because we didn't think Uncle Sam should be with our doc at the business end of the lady stirrups. Every ad hominem tool was employed against us, and while dissent was considered "patriotic" under the Bush administration, it was made outright criminal by the Obama admin. Government agencies acted as sentinels, seeking and destroying or making supremely difficult the lives and actions of numerous conservative groups and activists. Catherine Engelbrecht and the King Street Patriots were targeted, Dinesh D'Souza, James O'Keefe, the Richmond Tea Party, and numerous others were persecuted and engaged in lawfare. George Soros–funded sites like Media Matters put reporters on people beats—assigning them to listen to and follow certain high-profile activists and conservatives. Rather than act as some quasijournalistic review, as they falsely presented themselves, they served as the official dumping ground for opposition research and acted as the official water carriers for the DNC. They were the attack dogs for the Obama admin, going so far as to present hysterically libelous headlines as news. They practiced the LBJ art of accusations, particularly the "make them deny it" tactic.

". . . was that in both the Ohio and Nebraska primaries, back to back, McGovern was confronted for the first time with the politics of the rabbit-punch and the groin shot, and in both states he found himself dangerously vulnerable to this kind of thing. Dirty politics confused him. He was not ready for it—and especially not from his fine old friend Hubert Humphrey. Toward the end of the Nebraska campaign he was spending most of his public time explaining that he was Not for abortion on demand, Not for legalized marijuana, Not for unconditional amnesty . . . and his staff was becoming more and more concerned that their man had been put completely on the defensive.

This is one of the oldest and most effective tricks in politics. Every hack in the business has used it in times of trouble, and it has even been elevated to the level of political mythology in a story about one of Lyndon Johnson's early campaigns in Texas. The race was close and Johnson was getting worried. Finally he told his campaign manager to start a massive rumor campaign about his opponent's lifelong habit of enjoying carnal knowledge of his own barnyard sows. Wrote Hunter S. Thompson in *Fear and Loathing: On the Campaign Trail '72*:

> "C——, we can't get away calling him a pig-f**ker," the campaign manager protested. "Nobody's going to believe a thing like that."

"I know," Johnson replied. "But let's make the son-ofab*tch deny it."

In this new media landscape, a denial is a scalp, a ridiculously false story can plant just one seed of division. That's the goal: Chaos.

During the early 2016 primary fight I was completely repulsed to see certain conservative Web sites engage in yellow journalism. I don't believe in the objectivity of any media entity. Everyone has a bias. For instance, I'm biased toward limited government and Christian values. I freely admit it; that's the difference. I don't believe in an unbiased media; it's a joke. Media was never unbiased; it was never objective. It began in the United States when people like Ben Franklin wrote under pseudonyms to talk trash about people with whom he disagreed. Media was never more than the comments of a YouTube section, with rare, shining exceptions that do not serve as the rule. Media already compromises journalistic ethics by claiming objectivity. There is no such thing. But there is such a thing as honesty. You can be opinionated and be honest. They are not mutually exclusive traits. It's frustrating to see conservative outlets that claim to be some sort of media ombudsmen utilizing for ad dollars the exact same tactics that they criticize on their pages. As reader consumption changes, so too changes the media landscape. News consumers are busier than they were twenty years ago. New technologies meant to make lives easier have somehow made them more complicated. New media—and I don't mean blogs, I mean Instagram, Tumblr, Twitter, Facebook (the era of blogs is over and we're smack in the middle of the micromedia and viral narratives era)—are adapted perfectly to giving consumers the thirty-second headline they require to work with their busy schedules. As it has become harder to distinguish truth from fantasy in media, so too has it become difficult to follow the workings of the Washington cabal. Certain power-hungry members of the elected class ignore promises to allow other lawmakers forty-eight hours to digest a thousand-page bill before voting, others propose suspiciously redundant legislation, and others still push through so much at once that it's virtually impossible for lawmakers (to say nothing of their constituents) to keep their pace. Adding insult to injury, the party that conservatives support regularly to prevent government excess has helped to enable it, less than the other, but enable it all the same. This, coupled with the lack of appreciation given to conservatives who for decades filled ballot boxes with GOP votes, exploded for the second time in 2015. A new nationalist movement was born, different from patriotism; time will tell where this political furor will lead.

Donald Trump, with whom I had maintained a good relationship, reached out to me through his team and asked if I would be his surrogate in the media. I have an insufferable anti-authoritarian streak. No matter how much I may like a particular candidate, I could never be a politician's mouthpiece. It's not what I do. I replied to the staffer that I could be relied upon only to give credit and criticism when and where they are due; I could not offer anything more. It was a polite denial; I had nothing personally against Trump. He was a guest on my program a plethora of times. I just prefer not to be in someone's pocket. I won't speculate whether it was this or my disagreement with his remarks during the Planned Parenthood–versus–Center for Medical Progress fight that "Planned Parenthood does a lot of good for women too" on Fox one evening that created the divide between me and Trump's orbit, but a divide was evident shortly after, nonetheless. Months later, and after many had asked, I publicly explained in *National Review* why I personally could not support him. The response from what I can only believe to be the candidate's core supporters was eye-opening. Aside from being called every sexually derogatory name in the book, I was labeled a "cuckservative" and more as a result of my opinion. A few things: I don't work at *National Review*, my opinion is my own; Reagan called it his "favorite magazine"; and it never endorsed McCain, only Romney over McCain in 2008. I blast the Left every day on my programs, and anyone who has any familiarity with my programs' content knew that I was moving toward this position the more I read and the more I interviewed Trump. There are conservatives who are nationalists, but not every nationalist is a conservative, and I can only think that this segment of the electorate is where the bulk of the hatred originated. I felt as though that politicians were exploiting that infuriating, helpless anger so many (myself included) feel and trying to direct it toward a specific purpose that does not include limited-government principles. I don't apologize for my contribution to the consortium; it was reasoned, well thought out, and written with a civil tongue—most important, it was my opinion. Maybe not yours, maybe not hers or his, but mine. And because I'm a conservative, it's cool if we don't agree. What isn't cool are the people who feel that questioning someone's marriage or suggesting that they should be raped is in any way an acceptable response when confronted with diversity of thought. In America we may like our doctors but we can't keep them, we can't keep our land when the Bureau of Land Management comes knocking (particularly if you're a North Texas rancher), we can't keep illegal aliens from entering our country without being sued by the

DOJ, but we can still keep our opinions. (Well, some of us. Others have been prosecuted by the alphabet soup of bureaucratic agencies.)

I'm not perfect. I make mistakes. You can quite literally chart my political and spiritual growth online. I began writing about politics, pop culture, and lifestyle anonymously back in 2003, just another generic political blog, a dime a dozen. That turned into a newspaper column, through which I was offered a radio job in the spring of 2008. The rest is history. When I began I was angry. I still am, but with experience comes wisdom. You can't always be angry about the state of the world, you can't always yell when talking to listeners through the mic, and you can't always be that person who is perpetually ticked off, because it burns too much energy and makes everyone else feel miserable. Anger isn't a solution. It's a motivator, but not a plan of action. You can't win anything without a plan of action. If you're angry that you are out of Double Stuf Oreos, staring down your pantry and being mad about it doesn't put Oreos in your pantry. Being angry enough about it, wanting them badly enough that you'll drive to the store, buy some, and put them in the pantry yourself, well, that plan of action succeeds. You can be angry six ways to Sunday about the state of government, but being mad about it doesn't change it. Ranting on Facebook doesn't change it. Sending e-mails with the subject line "YOU SUCK!!1!!1" to conservative female talk-radio hosts who simply think differently about a primary candidate doesn't change it, either. In July of 2009 I spoke at a Tea Party rally in mid-Missouri. The Tea Party was total Americana. I've never seen a rally where people brought fold-up chairs, umbrella hats for the sun, and coolers full of Hi-C, but they did at Tea Party rallies. People said prayers and sang the national anthem at every rally I attended across the country. While there were such groups on the coasts, the fire came from the heartland. From Flyover Nation. I said at this rally that our fight is a marathon, not a sprint.

"Progressives have a generation on us," I told the crowd. "We cannot expect in one, two, or a few election cycles to match what they have accomplished with generations of plotting and misinformation." The struggle is slow, but we've made progress. We have more conservative senators and a conservative caucus in the House; Eric Cantor is out; Boehner is out. I am not yet satisfied, and neither is almost anyone else. There is still so much to do, so much that some of those same patriots who stood with me that day and said, "Yes! a marathon!" feel dispirited and have given up entirely, or given in to total anger. Please don't.

For many weeks I focused on Matthew 10:28:

Do not be afraid of those who kill the body but cannot kill the soul. Rather, be afraid of the One who can destroy both soul and body in hell.

What is the "soul" of conservatism? I have not faith in man over God but I have faith in the individual over government. I believe in the power of the individual over the power of government. I believe in voluntary stewardship of our fellow man, responsible stewardship of our country's affairs made possible only with the permission of the country's citizens. I believe in a strong national defense, really the government's only job, and when the government isn't focused on defense, it can stay out of everybody's lives. That, to me, as I have always known it, is conservatism. The largest body for this, for all intents and purposes, has been the Republican Party, though it has been threatened by the growing number of libertarians and independent conservatives. However, the Republican Party has been a poor body for the soul in recent years. The discussion becomes, then, do we sacrifice the body for the soul? Do we sacrifice the building for the mission? Do we continue to support the body with the belief that we can preserve the soul and achieve the mission, bit by bit, even if we must compromise certain principles to get there? All politics is compromise, but there is a point when compromise becomes suicide. The limit is ever changing. It's hard to know. This adds to the Flyover anger.

I asked a friend recently, when discussing this very subject, and I meant it in love, "Why have you not done more to change hearts and minds than to sit on Facebook or Twitter? Why have you not phone-banked, gone door to door, written letters to the editor, donated everything you could directly to the campaign you support?" In quite a few of my discussions with people across the country, many have not done this. It's hard work changing hearts and minds. It's hard facing the possibility of rejection or having to satisfy yourself with knowing that maybe your only victory that day was planting the seed. But know this: Truth lasts longer than propaganda. Persistence works. Even water wears down rock. Our children need to see us never giving up, never giving in, and they need to participate with you, because, as Reagan said, "Freedom is never more than one generation away from extinction."

I have said often that I think there are a number of conservatives who like the idea of limited government and the fist-in-the-air aesthetic of political incorrectness, but they also like to be comfortable. During the first Republican primary debate of the new year the veil was torn and the massive divide between

Flyover and the coasts revealed. Earlier in the primary Donald Trump jabbed Ted Cruz's faith and flamed the birther rumors by remarking, "Not a lot of evangelicals come from Cuba." Cruz returned fire, remarking, "Not a lot of conservatives come from New York." Trump defended his "New York values," at which point Cruz replied, "Everybody understands that the values in New York City are socially liberal and proabortion and pro–gay marriage and focus on money and the media." The coasts were apoplectic.

But why? Was that statement wrong? No, it wasn't.

Social media went crazy. It seemed like a competition to see who could win first place in butt-hurtness. But was Cruz wrong? New Yorkers are fleeing the state. Conservatives may congregate upstate, but they're outnumbered by Manhattan progressives. It's a state that has gone for Democrats by wide margins in the last seven presidential elections. When I hear "New York values," I think of the seven-round magazine limit, the ban on Big Gulps, de Blasio's disrespect of cops (remember when they turned their backs on him?), the New York SAFE Act criminalizing gun owners, the extra tax you have to pay just to have your bagel sliced at the deli, the fact that the New York City Council is barely elected, that gay hoteliers are attacked and treated like Elijah Lovejoy just short of death simply for throwing an event for a Republican candidate. (Some partisans wondered why Republicans would meet with gay supporters at all, as opposed to—what?—throwing them off rooftops like ISIS does? I'll take my direction on planting seeds and engaging those who don't think like you from Christ, thanks.) I think of Chuck Schumer, Hillary Clinton, restrictions, high cost of living, high taxation, and criminal-justice decay when I think of "New York values." Something was said about New York that was simple policy truth and people lost their minds. Someone once asked me in classic straw man style: "Dana, what if a presidential candidate had disrespected *your* home state?" Like how? Like saying that Missouri is hemorrhaging jobs to states with right-to-work laws? That St. Louis has one of the highest crime rates in the nation? That I had to move out of the city because gangs and drugs were moving in? That the mayor and the sheep of a police chief blamed law-abiding gun owners for the crimes of repeat offenders as a way to justify further gun restrictions in the city, making it harder for moms like me to defend myself? That the city's high cost of doing business, lack of population outside working hours, and corruption have destroyed any recovery? Please. Try being from Flyover Nation and then tell me how bad you have it. We're called "bitter clingers," hillbillies, rednecks; we're mocked for meth, Walmart, muddin', and more. This is a daily occurrence. And yet we don't make people pay extra to the state to cut a bagel, nor do we limit your magazine capacity, and people are leaving to move here, not Manhattan. We are slammed every single day by coastal snobs who liken St. Louis and all of Fly-over to a monolithic cow town where it's assumed that everyone has uncomfortably similar DNA. New Yorkers were appalled that a Texas senator stated the obvious about their state. These are people who attack and denigrate Flyover Nation, who applaud the president for referring to us as "bitter clingers" and mock us on *Saturday Night Live*. We're supposed to defend them with lies against the simply stated truth? When did the right embrace political correctness? We need to have some folks join Black Lives Matter in its "safe space."

I come from unapologetic southern-Missouri stock. I come from farmers, from good ol' boys, from home cookin', from the land of moonshine and coveralls, from people who would give you the shirt off their back if you needed it and a busted lip if you needed that too. I don't subscribe to lockstep, hive-mind thinking. Never have. Never will. I love God, family, and country, in that order. I love the principles with which I was raised, principles I saw in action when my single mom took three jobs to stay off the government dole, when my grandpa would come home of an evening from the fields with dirt on his jeans and grease on his hands. I saw these principles in action when my cousin volunteered to go to war right out of high school. I saw these principles when my aunts and uncles would argue and drama would ensue—until Grandma, the ultimate matriarch, shut it down with one single look. I saw these principles when my cousin walked her down the aisle to be seated at my wedding. I saw them again when I told her I was pregnant with her first great-grandchild and she patted my expanding belly and with the wisest smile I've ever seen replied, "I already knew, child." I saw them in my husband's grandmother, who emerged from the fog of Alzheimer's long enough to meet that baby, her great-grandson; a warm glow of recognition spread across her face as she cooed, "I know you!" while holding his tiny hands.

I felt them when I would sit on the porch swing with Grandpa, the first father figure I ever knew, and lay my head on his shoulder while his large, tobacco-stained fingers ran through my hair until I went to sleep. I saw them when my entire family held vigil for him at the VA, taking turns to make sure he was never, ever alone in the hospital. I saw them when my mother almost leaped across the nurses' desk at that same hospital, my aunts standing in solidarity behind her, after she discovered how long Grandpa and the other veterans had gone without water through the night. I saw those principles when I saw my grandfather cry or show emotion for the first time in my life at my grandmother's funeral as he collapsed near the casket in tears that could not be contained and every man in the family abandoned all formality and raced to be at his side.

I see them in people from my family's hometown and home county, people who don't know me but know my family name and display my magazine covers in their mom-and-pop shops and helped my stepdad gather copies of one magazine all across town to give away to friends. I saw it at my uncle's funeral, where I gave the eulogy, in the worn faces of people who'd fought through some hard things in life but were in tears before his casket as they realized the magnanimity of God.

I saw those principles and values in two ladies who came to one of my book signings and told me as I signed their books that they were from the Ozarks before departing with a "God bless you." I see it in my friends, good country folk like my friends Jimi Pirtle and the Kruta family, the latter of whom have had a family-owned bakery for generations and bring St. Louis Gooey Butter Cake for me and my entire staff whenever I'm in town. I saw these principles and values of compassion and love in my own boys one day when, while walking with them through Target, I suddenly realized I was alone. I looked back and saw them saluting and thanking a soldier in uniform, who shook their hands as his wife stood near their cart filled with diapers, cradling their infant in a sling. I see these principles still when my oldest son reminds me at a restaurant to bow my head for grace before he confidently and loudly thanks God for our blessings.

Whenever I feel lost and tempest tossed in this world, I think of these things. I think of Flyover Nation. These people and what they believe are the soul of this nation. "Bitter cling-ers?" Hardly. And FYI, "hillbilly" is a compliment. You'll be wishing you knew one if things get rough in the world.

Whenever I feel that they and their values are under attack, my eyebrow (my "Ozark eyebrow," as my friend Jimi calls it) raises and my nostrils flare. Whether I've met them or not, they're all family (and as big as my family is, heck, we might actually be related).

And they are angry and they feel unappreciated. Angry and unappreciated because they have become an increasingly iso-lated island in a country that values popularity, pocketbook, and power over principle. Unlike places like Washington, peo-ple in Flyover don't just get angry. They know anger isn't a solution or a plan of action; it's simply a motivator. And with a clenched jaw they'll roll up their sleeves and set out to change things. We can only hope.

Notes

Chapter One: You Can't Unfriend Family

1. Chad Bird, "The Tragic Death of the Funeral," *Federalist*, December 2013.
2. Brittany Maynard, "My Right to Death with Dignity at 29," CNN.com, November 2014.
3. "Letters: The Conservatives Should Leave Hunting Off Next Year's Election Manifesto," *Telegraph*, December 2014.
4. "The Country Where Death Is Now Just a Lifestyle Choice," *Daily Mail*, January 2015.
5. "Number of Mentally Ill Patients Killed by Euthanasia in Holland Trebles in a Year as Doctors Warn Assisted Suicide Is 'Out of Control,'" *Daily Mail*, October 2014.
6. "Police Confiscate Jars of Suspected Urine & Feces, Bricks, Tampons, Condoms from Protesters at Texas Capitol as Final Vote on Pro-Life Bill Nears," *Blaze*, July 2013.

Chapter Two: Against the Powers of This Dark World

7. "America's Changing Religious Landscape," Pew Research Center, May 2015.

8. "Congratulations, Leftists: You Shut Down Memories Pizza of Walkerton, IN," *Daily Caller*, April 2015.

9. "'Guilty as Charged,' Cathy Says of Chick-fil-A's Stand on Biblical & Family Values," *Baptist Press*, July 2012.

10. "Fayette Circuit Court Judge Reverses Finding in Hands On Originals Discrimination Case," *Lexington Herald Leader*, April 2015.

11. Associated Press, "Gay Couple Sue Hawaii B&B, Claim Discrimination," December 2011.

12. "Judge Rules Christian Facility Cannot Ban Same-Sex Civil Union Ceremony on Its Own Premises," *LifeSiteNews*, January 2012.

13. "Lesbian Couple Claims 'Mental Rape' at Refusal of Wedding Cake," DanaRadio.com, April 2015.

14. "Lesbian Couple Refused Wedding Cake Files State Discrimination Complaint," *Oregonian*, August 2013.

15. Ryan Roberts, Facebook post, April 3, 2015, www.facebook.com/ryanrobertsRR/posts/10102029654138723.

Chapter Three: Profiles in Pandering

16. Justin McCarthy, "Trust in Mass Media Returns to All-Time Low," *Gallup*, September 17, 2014, www.gallup.com/poll/176042/trust-mass-media-returns-time-low.aspx.

17. http://radaronline.com/exclusives/2012/08/highest-paid-anchors-matt-lauer-anderson-cooper-diane-sawyer/.

18. PricewaterhouseCoopers, "Cities of Opportunity: The Urban Rhythm of Entertainment and Media," February 2015, www.pwc.de/de/technologie-medien-und-telekommunikation/assets/pwc-cities-of-opportunity.pdf.

19. Martha's Vineyard Buyer Agents, "Martha's Vineyard Monthly Market Snapshot: Statistics for January 1, 2016 Through

January 31, 2016," www.mvbuyeragents.com/marthas-vineyard
-real-estate-trends.

20. http://www.dailymail.co.uk/news/article-2737802/Chelsea
    -Clinton-quits-600-000-year-role-special-correspondent-NBC
    .html#ixzz3BsQQ3rCA.

21. Richard Johnson, "Staff Quit Clinton Foundation over Chel-
    sea," *Page Six*, May 18, 2015, http://pagesix.com/2015/05/18/
    chelsea-sends-clinton-foundation-staff-running/.

22. http://www.newsbusters.org/blogs/cheri-jacobus/2014/06/23
    /nbcs-chelsea-clinton-i-dont-care-about-money-and-i-will
    -always-work-h.

23. Celebrity Net Worth, "Diane Sawyer Net Worth," www.celebrity
    networth.com/richest-celebrities/diane-sawyer-net-worth/.

24. Margo Howard, "*60 Minutes'* Newest Correspondent, Diane
    Sawyer," *People*, November 5, 1984, www.people.com/people/
    archive/article/0,20089065,00.html.

25. Bio, "Diane Sawyer Biography," www.biography.com/people/
    diane-sawyer-9472787#profile.

26. Howard, "*60 Minutes'* Newest Correspondent."

27. "Diane Sawyer: Good Morning Bias," *Media Research Center*,
    July 16, 2010, www.mrc.org/profiles-bias/diane-sawyer.

28. Scott Whitlock, "Liberal Diane Sawyer Swears Neutrality: 'People
    Will Know What the Truth Is,'" *MRC NewsBusters*, July 8, 2011,
    http://newsbusters.org/blogs/scott-whitlock/2011/07/08/liberal
    -diane-sawyer-swears-neutrality-people-will-know-what-truth.

29. Mary Meehan and Rich Copley, "Eastern Kentuckians Mixed
    on '20/20' Report," *Lexington Herald-Leader*, February 18,
    2009, www.kentucky.com/2009/02/18/697946/eastern
    -kentuckians-mixed-on-2020.html#storylink=cpy.

30. Don Kaplan, "Diane Sawyer Ends Five-Year Run as ABC's
    'World News' Anchor," *New York Daily News*, August 28,
    2014, www.nydailynews.com/entertainment/tv/diane-sawyer
    -sign-early-abc-world-news-article-1.1918875.

31. Shayna Jacobs, "Don Nichols' Will Splits His Estate Between Widow Diane Sawyer and His Three Children," *New York Daily News*, December 3, 2014, www.nydailynews.com /entertainment/movies/mike-nichols-leaves-fortune-diane -sawyer-article-1.2032142.

32. Stephen M. Silverman, "Inside Diane Sawyer and Mike Nichols's Longtime Romance," *People*, November 20, 2014, www.people .com/article/diane-sawyer-mike-nichols-romance-marriage.

33. Daniel Miller, "Why Hollywood Hides Out at Martha's Vineyard," *Hollywood Reporter*, August 6, 2011, www.holly woodreporter.com/news/why-hollywood-hides-at-marthas -220053.

34. Ibid.

35. Silverman, "Inside Diane Sawyer and Mike Nichols's Longtime Romance."

36. Steve Myrick, "Accomplished Film, Stage Director Mike Nichols, Dead at 83," *Martha's Vineyard Times*, November 20, 2014, www.mvtimes.com/2014/11/20/accomplished-film-stage -director-mike-nichols-dead-83/.

37. Bio, "George Stephanopoulos Biography," www.biography.com/ people/george-stephanopoulos-9542062#synopsis.

38. Pennebaker Hegedus Films, "The War Room," http://phfilms .com/films/the-war-room/.

39. Ibid.

40. John F. Harris, "Stephanopoulos Book Tests Loyalty," *Washington Post*, March 8, 1999, www.washingtonpost.com/wp-srv/ politics/special/clinton/stories/clinton030899.htm.

41. "George Stephanopoulos' Biography," *ABC News*, http:// abcnews.go.com/GMA/george-stephanopoulos-good-morning -america-anchor-biography/story?id=133369.

42. Celebrity Net Worth, "George Stephanopoulos Net Worth," www.celebritynetworth.com/richest-celebrities/george -stephanopoulos-net-worth/; Emily Smith, "ABC's 'Secret'

$105M Gamble on Stephanopoulos," *Page Six*, May 18, 2015, http://pagesix.com/2015/05/18/george-stephanopoulos-future-and-105m-contract-in-danger/.

43. Dylan Byers, "'Clinton Cash' Author Hits Stephanopoulos for 'Massive Breach of Ethical Standards,'" *Politico*, May 14, 2015, www.politico.com/blogs/media/2015/05/clinton-cash-author-hits-stephanopoulos-for-massive-breach-of-ethical-standards-207149.

44. Ibid.

45. Scott Whitlock, "George Stephanopoulos Hedges on Hillary Scandal: 'This Is a Tough One,'" *MRC NewsBusters*, April 29, 2015, http://newsbusters.org/blogs/scott-whitlock/2015/04/29/george-stephanopoulos-hedges-hillary-scandal-tough-one.

46. Ibid.

47. Dylan Byers, "Stephanopoulos Regrets Clinton Foundation Donation, Will Not Moderate GOP Debate," *Politico*, May 14, 2015, www.politico.com/blogs/media/2015/05/stephanopoulos-regrets-clinton-foundation-donation-will-not-moderate-gop-debate-207160#.VVTpm_9gdh0.twitter.

48. Kathryn Lofton, "My Take: How Oprah Became a Messiah," *CNN Belief Blog*, May 25, 2011, http://religion.blogs.cnn.com/2011/05/25/my-take-how-oprah-became-a-messiah/.

49. Stephanie Vozza, "Personal Mission Statements of 5 CEOs (and Why You Should Write One Too)," *Fast Company*, February 25, 2014, www.fastcompany.com/3026791/dialed/personal-mission-statements-of-5-famous-ceos-and-why-you-should-write-one-too.

50. Julie Zeveloff, "The FABULOUS Homes, Planes, and Other Toys of Oprah Winfrey," *Business Insider*, May 25, 2011, www.businessinsider.com/oprah-winfrey-houses-planes-2011-5?op=1.

51. Jake Braught, "The Most Ridiculous of Oprah's Favorite Things," *Article Cats*, January 7, 2015, http://articlecats.com/index.php/oprahs-most-ridiculous-favorite-things/.

52. Kate Spencer, "12 Gifts from Oprah's Favorite Things List That Remind Us That She's Oprah and We're Not," *Mommyish*,

November 4, 2014, http://www.mommyish.com/2014/11/04/
oprah-winfrey-favorite-things-list-2014/.

53. Tricia Romano, "Dr. Phil McGraw: Six Lawsuits and Scandals," *Daily Beast*, March 17, 2011, www.thedailybeast
.com/articles/2011/03/17/dr-phil-mcgraw-six-lawsuits-and-
scandals.html.

54. Associated Press, "$10.5M Settlement in Dr. Phil Diet Plan
Suit," Today.com, September 26, 2006, www.today.com/id/
15014778/ns/today-today_entertainment/t/m-settlement-dr
-phil-diet-plan-suit/#.VgAGSJ1VhBd.

55. Amanda Michelle Steiner, "Dr. Oz Speaks Out After Top
Physicians Demand His Dismissal from Columbia University,"
People, April 17, 2015, www.people.com/article/dr-oz-reaction
-doctors-demand-dismissal-columbia-university.

Chapter Four: Defending American Exceptionalism

56. Ruth Quinn, "Military Intelligence—This Week in History: 7
February 1967," Army.mil, January 31, 2013, www.army.mil
/article/95395/Military_Intelligence___this_week_in_history
__7_February_1967/.

57. "Medal of Honor, George Kenton Sisler," 307th Bomb
Wing B-47/KC-97 Association, www.307bwassoc.org/
sisler.htm.

58. "George Kenton (Ken) Sisler," Arkansas State University,
www.astate.edu/a/military-science/hall-of-heroes/george-kenton
-sisler/index.dot.

59. "Vietnam War Medal of Honor Recipients (M–Z)," Army.mil,
www.history.army.mil/html/moh/vietnam-m-z.html#SISLER.

60. Ibid.

61. Ibid.

62. Quinn, "Military Intelligence."

63. Ibid.

64. Ibid.

65. Richie Bernardo, "2015's Most and Least Patriotic States," *WalletHub*, https://wallethub.com/edu/most-and-least-patriotic -states/13680/.

66. Ibid.

67. Ibid.

68. Jeremy Bender, Andy Kiersz, and Armin Rosen, "Some States Have Much Higher Enlistment Rates Than Others," *Business Insider*, July 20, 2014, www.businessinsider.com/us-military-is -not-representative-of-country-2014-7.

69. http://newsoffice.duke.edu/all-about-duke/quick-facts-about -duke.

70. jb304@duke.edu, "Secretary Robert Gates," Duke University Program in American Grand Strategy, http://sites.duke.edu/agsp/ 2010/09/29/secretary-robert-gates/.

71. Shanea Watkins and James Sherk, "Who Serves in the U.S. Military? The Demographics of Enlisted Troops and Officers," Heritage Foundation, August 21, 2008, www.heritage.org /research/reports/2008/08/who-serves-in-the-us-military-the -demographics-of-enlisted-troops-and-officers.

72. Kathy Roth-Doquet, "Absence of America's Upper Classes from the Military," *ABC News*, http://abcnews.go.com/US/story?id= 2270473&page=1.

73. Ibid.

74. Ibid.

75. jb304@duke.edu, "Secretary Robert Gates."

76. Bender, Kiersz, and Rosen, "Some States Have Much Higher."

77. Benjamin Luxenberg, "If Inequality Is Our Problem, Military Service Is the Answer" (op-ed), *Los Angeles Times*, January 6, 2015, www.latimes.com/opinion/op-ed/la-oe-luxenberg -military-service-as-asset-20150107-story.html.

78. Watkins and Sherk, "Who Serves in the U.S. Military?"

79. Chuck Raasch, "Number of Veterans in Congress Has Fallen Drastically Since Post-Vietnam Years," *St. Louis Post-Dispatch*, May 26, 2014, www.stltoday.com/news/local/govt-and-politics /number-of-veterans-in-congress-has-fallen-drastically-since -post/article_bd824d5f-0a02-569c-91fc-0b7a62b6dab1.html.

80. Ibid.

81. Roth-Doquet, "Absence of America's Upper Classes."

82. James Ledbetter, "What Is American Exceptionalism?" *The Great Debate*, Reuters, January 23, 2012, http://blogs.reuters .com/great-debate/2012/01/23/what-is-american-exceptionalism/.

83. Ibid.

84. Howard Zinn, "The Power and the Glory," *Boston Review*, June 1, 2005, http://bostonreview.net/zinn-power-glory.

85. David Harsanyi, "Sorry Ron Fournier, Obama's Idea of American Exceptionalism Is Still Unexceptional," *The Federalist*, June 5, 2015, http://thefederalist.com/2015/06/05/sorry-ron-fournier -obamas-idea-of-american-exceptionalism-is-still-unexceptional/.

86. Robert Farley, "Obama and 'American Exceptionalism,'" FactCheck.org, February 15, 2015, www.factcheck.org/2015/ 02/obama-and-american-exceptionalism/.

87. John McCormack, "Obama Snobbery Watch," *Weekly Standard*, July 8, 2008, www.weeklystandard.com/weblogs/TWSFP/ 2008/07/obama_snobbery_watch.asp.

88. Ben Smith, "Obama on Small-Town Pa.: 'Clinging to Religion, Guns, Xenophobia,'" *Ben Smith Blog, Politico*, April 11, 2008, www.politico.com/blogs/ben-smith/2008/04/obama-on-small -town-pa-clinging-to-religion-guns-xenophobia-007737.

89. Victor David Hanson, "From Energy to Foreign Policy to the Presidency Itself, Obama's Agenda Rolls Along," *National Review*, October 1, 2013, www.nationalreview.com/article/ 359967/obama-transforming-america-victor-davis-hanson.

90. "Michelle Obama Takes Heat for Saying She's 'Proud of My Country' for the First Time," FoxNews.com, February 19, 2008,

www.foxnews.com/story/2008/02/19/michelle-obama-takes-heat
-for-saying-shersquos-lsquoproud-my-countryrsquo-for.html.

91. Hanson, "From Energy to Foreign Policy."

92. Jonathon M. Seidl, "What Did Michelle Obama Say to
the President During the 9/11 Ceremony (Take the Poll)," *Blaze*,
September 15, 2011, www.theblaze.com/stories/2011/09/15/
what-did-michelle-obama-say-to-the-president-during-the-911-
ceremony/.

Chapter Five: A Heart Problem and a Criminal-Justice Problem

93. Thomas John Belton to the Continental Congress, April 11, 1777.

94. Dana Loesch, *Hands Off My Gun* (Hachette, 2015); Bureau of
Justice Statistics, *National Crime Victimization Survey, 2000.*

95. Brian Ross, et al., "Secret US Policy Blocks Agents from Looking at Social Media of Visa Applicants, Former Official Says,"
ABC News, December 14, 2015, http://abcnews.go.com/US
/secret-us-policy-blocks-agents-social-media-visa/story?id=
35749325.

96. Justin Finch, et al., "Cops: Suspect Says He Shot Officer in
Name of Islam," *CBS Philly*, January 8, 2016, http://philadel
phia.cbslocal.com/2016/01/08/police-officer-shot-multiple-
times-in-west-philly/?utm_medium=twitter&utm_source=
twitterfeed.

97. "Philly Mayor: ISIS-Inspired Cop Shooting 'Had Nothing to Do
with Any Faith,'" *Fox News Insider*, January 9, 2016, http://
insider.foxnews.com/2016/01/09/philly-mayor-jim-kenney-cop
-shooting-had-nothing-do-any-faith.

98. Anna Orso, "Alleged Cop Shooter Edward Archer Pleaded
Guilty to a 2012 Armed Assault," *Billy Penn*, January 8, 2016,
http://billypenn.com/2016/01/08/alleged-cop-shooter-edward
-archer-pleaded-guilty-to-a-2012-armed-assault/.

99. www.ksdk.com/story/news/local/2014/11/18/vonderrit-myers
-case-prompts-new-questions-about-gps-monitoring/19250197/.

100. Jennifer Meckles, "Vonderrit Myers Case Prompts Questions About GPS Monitoring," KSDK.com, November 18, 2014, www.kmov.com/news/crime/Mayor-police-chief—288845131.html.

101. Caroline May, "Biden to NRA: We 'Don't Have the Time' to Prosecute Gun Buyers Who Lie on Background Checks," *Daily Caller*, January 18, 2013, http://dailycaller.com/2013/01/18/biden-to-nra-we-dont-have-the-time-to-prosecute-people-who-lie-on-background-checks/.

102. https://www.washingtonpost.com/news/powerpost/wp/2015/12/03/senate-democrats-to-force-gun-control-votes-in-the-wake-of-the-san-bernardino-shooting/.

103. Bureau of Alcohol, Tobacco, and Firearms, "How May an Unlicensed Person Receive a Firearm in His or Her State That He or She Purchased from an Out-of-State Source?," last reviewed February 10, 2016, www.atf.gov/questions-and-answers/qa/how-may-unlicensed-person-receive-firearm-his-or-her-state-he-or-she.

104. Eli Lake and Audrey Hudson, "Napolitano Stands By Controversial Report," *Washington Times*, April 16, 2009, www.washingtontimes.com/news/2009/apr/16/napolitano-stands-rightwing-extremism/?page=all.

105. Dana Loesch, "Whose Name Tops the MIAC Report?" *The Dana Show*, October 15, 2012, http://danaloeschradio.com/news/whose-name-tops-the-miac-report.

106. Loesch, *Hands Off My Gun*.

107. Alissa Tabirian, "CDC Study: Use of Firearms for Self-Defense Is 'Important Crime Deterrent,'" CNSNews.com, July 17, 2013, www.cnsnews.com/news/article/cdc-study-use-firearms-self-defense-important-crime-deterrent.

108. Jens Manuel Krogstad, "Gun Homicides Steady After Decline in '90s; Suicide Rate Edges Up," *Pew Research Center*, October 21, 2015, www.pewresearch.org/fact-tank/2015/10/21/gun-homicides-steady-after-decline-in-90s-suicide-rate-edges-up/.

Chapter Six: Professional Agitators

109. Monica Davey and Manny Fernandez, "Security in Ferguson Is Tightened After Night of Unrest," *New York Times*, November 25, 2014, http://www.nytimes.com/2014/11/26/us/ferguson -missouri-violence.html?_r=0.

110. Christopher Bucktin, "Ferguson Riots: Unrest Across US as Violence 'Much Worse' Than Protests Following Michael Brown's Death," *Mirror*, November 25, 2014, http://www .mirror.co.uk/news/world-news/ferguson-riots-unrest-across- violence-4696025.

111. "Hired Black Lives Matter Protesters Start #CutTheCheck After Being Stiffed by ACORN Successor Group," *Newsmax*, May 2015.

112. Chris Hayes, "One Man's Protests Push Police to the Limit," *Fox 2 Now*, October 23, 2014, http://fox2now.com/2014/10/23/ one-mans-protests-push-police-to-the-limit/.

113. Andrew Soergel, "Sharpton: 'America, It's Time to Deal with Policing,'" *U.S. News and World Report*, August 25, 2014, http://www.usnews.com/news/newsgram/articles/2014/08/25 /al-sharpton-speaks-at-ferguson-teen-michael-browns-funeral -in-st-louis.

114. Lilly Workneh, "Al Sharpton Calls Ferguson Grand Jury Decision 'Expected, But Still an Absolute Blow,'" *Huffington Post*, November 25, 2014, http://www.huffingtonpost.com/ 2014/11/25/al-sharpton-ferguson_n_6215716.html.

115. "President Obama Defends Black Lives Matter Movement," *CBS News*, October 23, 2015, http://www.cbsnews.com/ news/president-barack-obama-defends-black-lives-matter- movement/.

116. Tina Moore, et al., "Two NYPD Officers 'Assassinated' While Sitting in Patrol Car in Brooklyn by Gunman Who Boasted on Instagram About 'Revenge' Killing Cops," *New York Daily*

News, December 21, 2014, http://www.nydailynews.com
/new-york/nyc-crime/cops-shot-brooklyn-sources-article
-1.2051941.

117. Bob McManus, "There Is Blood on Hands of Those Who
Demanded 'Dead Cops,'" *New York Post*, December 14, 2014,
http://nypost.com/2014/12/21/there-is-blood-on-hands-of-those
-who-demanded-dead-cops/.

118. Wesley Lowery, "Protest Leaders Seek to Distance Budding
Movement from New York Police Killings," *Washington Post*,
December 21, 2014, https://www.washingtonpost.com/national
/protest-leaders-seek-to-distance-budding-movement-from-new
-york-police-killings/2014/12/21/3ede9b1c-8948-11e4-8ff4
-fb93129c9c8b_story.html.

119. Kelly Riddell, "George Soros Funds Ferguson Protests, Hopes to
Spur Civil Action," *Washington Times*, January 14, 2015, http://
www.washingtontimes.com/news/2015/jan/14/george-soros
-funds-ferguson-protests-hopes-to-spur/?page=all.

120. Chuck Ross, "Black Lives Matter Protesters Chant: 'Pigs in a
Blanket, Fry 'Em Like Bacon,'" *Daily Caller*, August 29, 2015,
http://dailycaller.com/2015/08/29/black-lives-matter-protesters
-chant-pigs-in-a-blanket-fry-em-like-bacon-video/.

121. Manny Fernandez and David Montgomery, "Texas Deputy
Killed 'Because He Wore a Uniform,' Sheriff Says," *New York
Times*, August 29, 2015, http://www.nytimes.com/2015/08/30
/us/shooting-of-texas-deputy-is-called-coldblooded-execution
.html?smid=tw-share.

122. Chuck Ross, "Following Execution of Deputy, Officials Con-
demn 'Open Warfare' on Cops," *Daily Caller*, August 29, 2015,
http://dailycaller.com/2015/08/29/following-execution-of-
deputy-officials-condemn-open-warfare-on-cops-video/.

123. Ibid.

124. Fernandez and Montgomery, "Texas Deputy Killed 'Because He
Wore a Uniform.'"

Chapter Seven: Degrading Yourself and Calling It Equality

125. Ashe Schow, "Columbia Student Found 'Not Responsible' of Rape Finally Tells His Side of the Story," *Washington Examiner*, February 4, 2015, www.washingtonexaminer.com/columbia -student-found-not-responsible-of-rape-finally-tells-his -side-of-the-story/article/2559742.

126. Ashe Schow, "Columbia Student Accused of Rape Amends Lawsuit to Include 'the Mattress Attends Graduation,'" *Washington Examiner*, July 22, 2015, www.washingtonexaminer.com/ columbia-student-accused-of-rape-amends-lawsuit-to-include-the- mattress-attends-graduation/article/2568763.

127. Katherine Timpf, "Students Told to Take Photos with a 'Consent Contract' Before They Have Sex," *National Review*, July 7, 2015, www.nationalreview.com/article/420870/college -affirmative-consent-contract.

128. Gretel C. Kovach, "Marines: Women Fare Worse in Combat Skills Tests," *San Diego Union-Tribune*, September 10, 2015, www.sandiegouniontribune.com/news/2015/sep/10/marines -women-in-combat-task-force-results/.

129. Rowan Scarborough, "Pressure Grows on Marines to Consider Lowering Combat Standards for Women," *Washington Times*, April 19, 2015, www.washingtontimes.com/news/2015/apr/19/ marine-corps-weighs-lower-standards-for-women-afte/?page=all.

130. Christina Hoff Sommers, "No, Women Don't Make Less Money Than Men," *Daily Beast*, February 1, 2014, www.thedailybeast .com/articles/2014/02/01/no-women-don-t-make-less-money -than-men.html.

131. Sarah Ketterer, "The 'Wage Gap' Myth That Won't Die," *Wall Street Journal*, September 30, 2015, www.wsj.com/articles/ the-wage-gap-myth-that-wont-die-1443654408.

132. Mark J. Perry and Andrew G. Biggs, "The '77 Cents on the Dollar' Myth About Women's Pay," *Wall Street Journal*, April 7,

2014, www.wsj.com/articles/SB10001424052702303532704579
483752909957472.

133. Matthew Rousu, "Childless Women in Their Twenties Out-Earn Men. So?" *Forbes*, February 24, 2014, www.forbes.com/sites /realspin/2014/02/24/childless-women-in-their-twenties-out -earn-men-so/.

134. Nolan Feeney, "Women Are Now More Likely to Have College Degree Than Men," *Time*, October 7, 2015, http://time.com/ 4064665/women-college-degree/.

135. David French, "Victim Culture Is Killing American Manhood," *National Review*, September 29, 2015.

136. Sarah Boesveld, "Becoming Disabled by Choice, Not Chance: 'Transabled' People Feel Like Impostors in Their Fully Working Bodies," *National Post*, June 3, 2015, http://news.nationalpost .com/news/canada/becoming-disabled-by-choice-not-chance -transabled-people-feel-like-impostors-in-their-fully-working -bodies#__federated=1.

Chapter Eight: Forgetting Who We Are

137. Brian Lombardi, "27 Ways to Be a Modern Man," *New York Times*, September 29, 2015.

138. David Edelstein, "Jesus H. Christ," *Slate*, February 24, 2004.

139. David Catron, "Republicans and Women's Rights: A Brief Reality Check," *American Spectator*, April 30, 2012, http:// spectator.org/articles/35608/republicans-and-womens-rights -brief-reality-check.

Chapter Nine: Conserving What We Have

140. Environmental Protection Agency, "Reorganization Plan No. 3 of 1970," July 9, 1920, www.epa.gov/aboutepa/reorganization -plan-no-3-1970.

141. Ibid.

142. https://books.google.com/books?id=Y_dVaJ7x-7QC&pg=
PA51&lpg=PA51&dq="The+ban+on+DDT+may+have+killed+
20+million+children.")&source=bl&ots=XN8qDJc5fN&sig=
AyQqXOGZ-ezyeZxcD7TBk-mvaI8&hl=en&sa=X&ved=
0ahUKEwjXt7rXg8fLAhVJZCYKHfrDCFUQ6AEINTAD#v=
onepage&q="The%20ban%20on%20DDT%20may%20have%
20killed%2020%20million%20children.")&f=false.

143. Mark Hendrickson, "The EPA: The Worst of Many Rogue
Federal Agencies," *Forbes*, March 14, 2013, www.forbes.com
/sites/markhendrickson/2013/03/14/the-epa-the-worst-of-many
-rogue-federal-agencies/#2715e4857a0b1f4262865beb.

144. Ibid.

145. Ibid.

146. Mark Hendrickson, "The EPA: The Worst of Many Rogue
Federal Agencies, Part II," *Forbes*, March 21, 2013, www
.forbes.com/sites/markhendrickson/2013/03/21/the-epa-the
-worst-of-many-rogue-federal-agencies-part-ii/#2715e4857a
0b953126d7a383.

147. Hendrickson, "The EPA: The Worst of Many Rogue Federal
Agencies," March 14, 2013.

148. Associated Press, "House Panel Targets 'Glaring Management
Failures' at EPA," *Fox News*, April 30, 2015, www.foxnews
.com/politics/2015/04/30/house-panel-targets-glaring
-management-failures-at-epa.html.

149. Ibid.

150. Ibid.

151. Joel Gehrke, "EPA's Lisa Jackson Resigning as Secondary Email
Investigation Begins," *Washington Examiner*, December 27,
2012, www.washingtonexaminer.com/epas-lisa-jackson-
resigning-as-secondary-email-investigation-begins/article/
2516938.

152. Jonathan Easley, "Obama Says His Is 'Most Transparent
Administration' Ever," *The Hill*, February 14, 2014, http://

thehill.com/blogs/blog-briefing-room/news/283335-obama
-this-is-the-most-transparent-administration-in-history.

153. "Obama's Nomination Victory Speech in St. Paul," *Huffington Post*, November 5, 2008, www.huffingtonpost.com/2008/06/03/obamas-nomination-victory_n_105028.html.

154. Michael Bastasch, "Flashback 2008: Obama Promised to 'Bankrupt' Coal Companies," *Daily Caller*, August 3, 2015, http://dailycaller.com/2015/08/03/flashback-2008-obama -promised-to-bankrupt-coal-companies/.

155. Amanda Carpenter, "Coal Company Cuts 500 Jobs, Blames Environmentalists," *Washington Times*, December 9, 2009, www.washingtontimes.com/blog/back-story/2009/dec/9/coal-company-cuts-500-jobs-blames-environmentalist/.

156. Patrice Hill, "Coal-Mining Jobs 'in Free-fall' After EPA Regs," *Washington Times*, June 12, 2014, www.washingtontimes.com/news/2014/jun/12/coal-mining-jobs-free-fall-after-epa-regs/.

157. Michael Bastasch, "Coal Mining Industry Sheds Tens of Thousands of Jobs Under Obama," *Daily Caller*, February 6, 2015, http://dailycaller.com/2015/02/06/coal-industry-sheds -tens-of-thousands-of-jobs-under-obama/.

158. Ibid.

159. Hill, "Coal-Mining Jobs 'in Free-fall.'"

160. Sam Batkins, "On Jobs and Regulations: In Graphs," *American Action Forum*, February 4, 2015, http://americanactionforum .org/insights/on-jobs-and-regulation-in-graphs.

161. "Clinton's Coal Reparations," *Wall Street Journal*, November 13, 2015, www.wsj.com/articles/clintons-coal-reparations -1447459569?alg=y.

Chapter Ten: Our Leaders Hate Us

162. Philip Blum, "In His New Job, Eric Cantor Will Make 26 Times the Average Household Income of His Old District,"

Washington Post, September 2, 2014, www.washingtonpost
.com/news/the-fix/wp/2014/09/02/eric-cantors-new-job-by-the-
numbers/.

163. Carol Morello, "The D.C. Suburbs Dominate the List of
Wealthiest U.S. Counties," *Washington Post*, December 12,
2103, www.washingtonpost.com/blogs/govbeat/wp/2013/12/12/
the-d-c-suburbs-dominate-the-list-of-wealthiest-u-s-counties/.

164. Jonathan Martin, "Lacking a House, a Senator Is Renewing His
Ties in Kansas," *New York Times*, February 7, 2014, www.nytimes
.com/2014/02/08/us/senator-races-to-show-ties-including-an
-address-in-kansas.html?_r=0.

165. Dan Carden, "Board Rules Lugar Not Eligible to Vote in
Indiana," *NWI Times*, March 15, 2012, www.nwitimes.com
/news/local/govt-and-politics/elections/board-rules-lugar-not
-eligible-to-vote-in-indiana/article_d227f50d-fa55-515e-b615
-fa610abbf066.html.

166. Philip Rucker, "Landrieu Claims Parents' Home as Her Own,
Raising Questions of Louisiana Residency," *Washington Post*,
August 24, 2014, www.washingtonpost.com/politics/landrieu
-claims-parents-home-as-her-own-raising-questions-of-louisiana
-residency/2014/08/28/423d8552-2e08-11e4-9b98-848790384093
_story.html.

167. Manu Raju, "Reid: Ritz-Carlton Not Home," *Politico*, October
21, 2010, www.politico.com/story/2010/10/reid-ritz-carlton-not
-home-043989.

168. Anna Palmer and Jake Sherman, "D.C.'s Tower of Power," *Politico*, April 10, 2015, www.politico.com/story/2015/04/harry
-reid-tom-daschle-ritz-carlton-residences-power-brokers-116827.

169. John Kelly, "Washington Built on a Swamp? Think Again,"
Washington Post, April 1, 2012, www.washingtonpost.com/
local/washington-built-on-a-swamp-think-again/2012/03/31/
gIQA7BfBpS_story.html.

170. "Tourist Guide: Mysteries of the Nation's Capital," *Washington Times*, May 20, 2009, www.washingtontimes.com/news/2009/ may/20/mysteries-of-the-nations-capital/?page=all.

171. Associated Press, "President Marks His First Year," *New York Times*, January 21, 1982, www.nytimes.com/1982/01/21/ business/president-marks-his-first-year.html.

172. Tim Carman, "If D.C.'s Steakhouse Days Are Over, Why Do So Many New Ones Keep Opening?" *Washington Post*, August 7, 2015, www.washingtonpost.com/lifestyle/food/if-dcs -steakhouse-days-are-over-why-do-so-many-new-ones-keep -opening/2015/08/07/9a9672ee-29a3-11e5-a250-42bd81 2efc09_story.html.

173. "Lobbying Database," OpenSecrets.org, www.opensecrets.org/ lobby/.

174. Architect of the U.S. Capitol, "U.S. Capitol Visitor Center," www.aoc.gov/capitol-buildings/us-capitol-visitor-center.

175. "Reid: Capitol Visitor Center Will Minimize 'Smell' of Tourists," *Fox News*, December 2, 2008, www.foxnews.com/politics/2008/ 12/02/reid-capitol-visitor-center-minimize-smell-tourists/.

176. Ibid.

177. United States Senator for Nevada Harry Reid, "About Senator Harry Reid," www.reid.senate.gov/about.

178. Alex Rogers, "3 Surprising Facts About Senator Harry Reid," *Time*, March 27, 2015, http://time.com/3761553/harry-reid -retire-things-you-should-know/.

179. United States Senator for Nevada Harry Reid, "About Senator Harry Reid."

180. Ibid.

181. Adam O'Neal, "Harry Reid's Long, Steady Accretion of Power & Wealth," *RealClearPolitics*, April 24, 2014, www.realclear politics.com/articles/2014/04/24/harry_reids_long_steady_ accretion_of_power__wealth.html.

182. Ibid.

183. Ibid.

184. Ibid.

185. Betsy Woodruff, "How Did Harry Reid Get Rich?" *National Review*, August 15, 2012, www.nationalreview.com/article/314025/how-did-harry-reid-get-rich-betsy-woodruff.

186. O'Neal, "Harry Reid's Long, Steady Accretion."

187. http://www.newsmax.com/Morris/US-Toyota-Consumer-Reports/2010/04/13/id/355530/.

188. O'Neal, "Harry Reid's Long, Steady Accretion."

189. Woodruff, "How Did Harry Reid Get Rich?"

190. Palmer and Sherman, "D.C.'s Tower of Power."

191. Woodruff, "How Did Harry Reid Get Rich?"

192. Alan Silverleib, "Senate Approves Health Care Reform Bill," *CNN*, December 24, 2009, www.cnn.com/2009/POLITICS/12/24/health.care/.

193. Charles Hurt, "Schumer Calls Flight Attendant Who Told Him to Turn Off Cell Phone 'Bitch,'" *New York Post*, December 16, 2009, http://nypost.com/2009/12/16/schumer-calls-flight-attendant-who-told-him-to-turn-off-cell-phone-bitch/.

194. Dan Amira, "Chuck Schumer Said a Not-Nice Thing About a Flight Attendant," *New York*, December 16, 2009, http://nymag.com/daily/intelligencer/2009/12/chuck_schumer_said_a_not_nice.html#.

195. Justin Bachman, "How Much Money Do Flight Attendants Make?" *BloombergBusiness*, December 27, 2013, www.bloomberg.com/news/articles/2013-12-27/everyone-wants-to-be-a-flight-attendant.

196. Toby Harnden, "The Most Influential US Liberals: 40–21," *Telegraph*, January 14, 2010, www.telegraph.co.uk/news/worldnews/northamerica/usa/6981433/The-most-influential-US-liberals-40-21.html.

197. Lynn Sweet, "Obama, McCain Comedy Riffs; Obama Middle Name Really 'Steve' Transcripts," *Chicago Sun-Times*, October

16, 2008, http://blogs.suntimes.com/sweet/2008/10/obama
_comedy_rift_middle_name.html.

198. http://www.nytimes.com/2014/12/17/us/after-decades
-lawmakers-are-roommates-no-more.html?_r=0.

199. Rent Jungle, "Rent Trend Data in Washington, District of
Columbia," www.rentjungle.com/average-rent-in-washington
-rent-trends/.

200. http://www.nytimes.com/2014/12/17/us/after-decades
-lawmakers-are-roommates-no-more.html?_r=0.

201. "Sen. Charles E. Schumer," OpenSecrets.org, www.opensecrets
.org/politicians/summary.php?cycle=Career&type=C&cid=
N00001093&newMem=N.

202. M. J. Lee, "Wall Street Welcomes Expected Chuck Schumer
Promotion," *CNN*, March 27, 2015, www.cnn.com/2015/03/27/
politics/chuck-schumer-business-wall-street/.

203. Hurt, "Schumer Calls Flight Attendant."

204. Ibid.